Daughters

of the

KING

Daughters
of the
KING

Written and created by
ERIKA FERGERSON CARROLL

ELF Visions

Daughters of the King
2nd Edition

ELF Visions
Daughters of the King
Copyright ©2022 by Erika Fergerson Carroll
Request for information should be addressed to:
ELF Visions email: elfvisioned@yahoo.com

Library of Congress Cataloging-in-Publication Data
Names: Fergerson Carroll, Erika, author.
Title: The Daughters of the King/ Erika Fergerson Carroll
Identifiers: LCCN 2022916024 (Print) ISBN: 978-1-7361404-7-5 (Hardcover)
ISBN: 978-1-7361404-8-2 (ebook)

Scripture quotations marked ESV or taken from the ESV® Bible (The Holy Bible, English Standard Version® (ESV®) Copyright © 2001 by Crossway, a publishing ministry of Good News Publishers. All rights reserved.

Unless otherwise noted. Scripture quotations taken from The Holy Bible, New International Version®, NIV® Copyright © 1973, 1978, 1984, 2011 by Biblica, Inc.® Used by permission. All rights reserved worldwide.

Scripture quotations marked NKJV or taken from the Holy Bible, New King James Version. Copyright © 1982 by Thomas Nelson,
Inc. Used by permission. All rights reserved."

All rights reserved. No part of this book may be reproduced or transmitted in any form or by any means, electronic or mechanical, including photocopying, recording, or by an information storage and retrieval system - except by a reviewer who may quote brief passages in a review to be printed in a magazine or newspaper - without permission in writing from the publisher.

Cover Design: Tharanga Kuruppu
Cover Photography: Trenton Fergerson
Cover Model: Shaznee Pittman
Interior Design: Mahabub Alam
Editor: Sheila Mills Carroll **Contact Information:**skiyewriter@gmail.com

🌷 Dedication 🌷

I dedicate this book to all women, who have experienced, who are experiencing and will experience the consequences and repercussions of horrible decision-making. Despite the season that you are enduring, please always remember that nothing can separate you from the love of Christ. You are not alone! He is the answer to any and every dilemma you may face and is always ready and available to welcome you back home with open arms. Daughters of the King, be blessed, refreshed, and encouraged!

God you are so amazing to me! Thank you for the heartaches and disappointments that drew me closer to you! I am so thankful that you, Lord God Almighty, give beauty for ashes. Thank you to my husband Anthony Carroll, my children, Blaise, sisters and parents for your encouragement and support! Also, thank you Andrea for supporting me in all of my kingdom endeavors. Sheila Mills Carroll thank you for your time, support and pouring yourself out to assist with the vision the Lord has given me! Thank you Pastor John K. Jenkins and First Lady Trina Jenkins for offering classes at First Baptist Church of Glenarden and teachers that allowed me to creatively express my biblical understanding of the Word. I love you and am grateful for all of you!

God bless you immensely,

Erika

Table of Contents

Introduction 1

Chapter 1: Don't Throw Stones 5

Chapter 2: Take Care Of Home 9

Chapter 3: Eye Patch Needed 15

Chapter 4: Killing Me Softly 27

Chapter 5: Don't Sleep On It 35

Chapter 6: Oops, I Bumped My Head 43

Chapter 7: My Guilty Pleasure 47

Chapter 8: Run Joe 57

Chapter 9: What In The Hell 65

Chapter 10: Beat It 73

Chapter 11: Loving You 81

Chapter 12: Fight The Power 87

Chapter 13: Self-Destruction 95

Chapter 14: No, No, No, No, No 103

Chapter 15: You So Evil 109

Chapter 16: Create In Me A Clean Heart 119

Chapter 17: I Ain't Ready 125

Chapter 18: Help A Sistah Out 131

Chapter 19: A Spoonful of Medicine 137

Chapter 20: Don't Judge Me 145

Chapter 21: You Must Not Know About Me 155

Chapter 22: Saved By the Bell 165

Chapter 23: Just A Slipping and Backsliding 177

Chapter 24: But You Don't Know The Cost 183

Chapter 25: Saving A Wretch Like Me 199

A Queen's Reflection 203

Daughters of the King Tract 207

Introduction

Our female ancestors have experienced many trials and tribulations that we endure today but understand that healing for our souls is an essential part for our wholeness. Daughters of the King is that tool that will assist in helping us to overcome! Daughters of The King familiarizes us with women's stories of the Bible itself, but with in-depth focus on modern day issues that women encounter. This 21st century book of biblical stories relates to present day adversities with an interesting ministerial approach and allows women readers to see the similarities between them and the women of the Bible. Love, abuse, rape, adultery, health issues, relational issues, and a multitude of other issues that women experience are discussed in the Daughters of The King series. As we read in Daughters of The King about the biblical women's disobedient choices as well as the consequences, we are reminded that as women that we fall down but can definitely get up again.

I am one of those women who has fallen numerous times just like the women you will read about in Daughters of The King. I am just a disciple chic straight out of the heart of Capitol Heights, Maryland who loves the Lord. All my life, I had to fight (shout out to Sofia from the Color Purple) to loving myself after being disappointed by men. Negative thoughts intruded my mind with that rattled my mind resulting from bad relationships as well as the deficiencies that bound my soul due to failed attempts to fill my voids. These are the catalysts that qualify me to write this book. The pain and tears that I have cried over the years caused by terrible decisions that I have made allows me to relate to the hurt and trauma that we as woman experience. We all want to be loved and when we open ourselves up to receive love without it been reciprocated properly is heart wrenching. Yes, I have had my share of sleepless nights after being rejected by my so called lovers. From those places, I have drawn into the open arms of the perfect lover of my soul. My desire for writing this book is to inform you, Sis, that you are not alone. Queen, I need you to understand that what you have experienced, are currently experiencing or will experience are the same issues that women have endured since the beginning of time and you are not by yourself! I believe the reason I endured my trials and tribulations in some of my relationships was for such a time as this. My prayer is that this book here, Daughters of The King, will make you laugh, affirm you, make you self-reflect, help you realize yourself worth, loose shackles, heal you and make you whole all by drawing you closer to God. Remember, I don't care how far you have fallen, you are still a Daughter of the King and nothing can separate you from his love!

Chapter 1

Don't Throw Stones

"For all have sinned and fall short of the glory of God," -Romans 3:23 NKJV

Women are in a correctional facility in Washington, D.C. watching the news on television, and the news highlights a shooting involving a woman in her 20's who was caught up in a crime of passion.

"It makes me truly upset to see women getting caught up because of a dude. I hope she is ok and doesn't end up in this joint," Cassandra expresses emphatically and with a look of deep concern.

"Yeah, I know what you are saying. I enjoy the group counseling sessions that they offer here. They keep me encouraged while doing this time. Our next meeting is at 2:00 p.m. today. You should really join us, Cassandra. It's extremely helpful. You should come," Niecy says while patting her itchy head.

"It sounds like it. I think I'll check it out. I just hope the counselors aren't judgmental and think that they are better than us. 'Cus, I ain't up for that. I'm just not," Cassandra states as she defiantly crosses her hands.

"No, you have the wrong impression. The counselors are down to earth and it seems to me like they genuinely care about us. I look forward to attending the weekly sessions. It's my weekly fix that keeps me going, especially on days when I get depressed. I assure you that you will like it," Niecy testifies while patting Cassandra's hand.

"Well, since you are positive that the energy will benefit me I will check it out today," Cassandra says willingly as she nods and unfolds her hands.

"Yep, it's starts at 2:00. I will see you there," Niecy grins as she points at Cassandra. In the auditorium, the chairs were set up in a circular fashion with inmates setting up more chairs for the participants as needed. Cassandra walked in a few minutes after 2:00. Niecy waved to grab Cassandra's attention to sit in the empty seat beside her. Deborah, 45 years old, with thick long natural hair, was in the middle of the circle of chairs and walked in circles as she spoke.

"Hello, Queens! I am glad that you took this opportunity to join me today. I see some new faces that I haven't seen before. Well for all of you who don't know who I am, I am Deborah. I am a retired judge that comes here in my spare time to encourage you. Although, I have the degree and accolades of being a judge, I am not judgmental in this space. I am here because I care and want you to make better choices. I want you to know that you are not alone. Ok, that's enough about me. Let's get started. Tell us your name and a little bit of your story but only if you feel comfortable enough to share," Deborah says in a welcoming tone directed toward Cassandra.

Cassandra stood up with a bold look on her face with her head tilted to the side while looking at Deborah straight in the eyes.

"Hello! My name is Cassandra. I am here.....I am here because I loved a man, and I chose to make some poor decisions. I was a selfish hoe at times and I was just straight gangsta with my lifestyle," Cassandra confesses with her eyes and head directed toward Deborah.

"Hmmm, I see! Thank you for sharing, Queen. Remember you're not the only one who has sinned and fallen short of the glory of God," Deborah grins as she looks at Cassandra straight in the eyes fearlessly.

The inmates cheer, clap and encourage Cassandra. Deborah pulls up a chair and squeezes in between two inmates.

"Cassandra, once again, beloved, you are not alone. In fact, none of you are by yourself when it comes to making poor decisions at times. That is why I am also a part of your circle. In fact, my mission is to decrease the staggering numbers of women who are currently imprisoned. Now, we all know a man can make you do some crazy things sometimes which can bring some unwanted outcomes. Now, I'm just saying. Listen, I am about to take you on a journey that highlights women who made some very poor decisions. As I dive into these, the insights of these queens' stories will be revealed. If you are honest, you may see a little bit of yourself in the lives of these women. Hmmmm, I think I will start from the beginning," Deborah dramatically explains with bright eyes and expressive hand movements.

Deborah begins to narrate the story.

Chapter 2

Take Care Of Home

"Husbands, love your wives"
-Ephesians 5:25 NKJV

Eve's Father's Garden

There is an assortment of vegetables in the garden including a large tree with large luscious red apples on its limbs. The Father, a wise older gentleman with a distinctively deep voice, is tending to his garden with his face unseen. He has large hands and is wearing Timberland boots covered in dirt from working in the garden. Young Eve is a 25 year old timid women with a pure heart. She has a dark coffee complexion and a shapely figure. Eve is married to Adam, a fine tall 25 year old brotha' with a chiseled body and a tantalizing Reese's cup complexion. Eve meets The Father in the garden to help him and to pick up some fresh veggies for Gabriella's restaurant.

"Eve you are a great helper. I know Adam surely appreciates you. He must be at work smiling joyfully."

"You know it," she speaks slowly with a tight forced smile.

Eve changes subjects quickly while pulling the weeds from the garden. Full of emotion, she stops tending to the garden and looks up at The Father.

"Daddy, your garden is so beautiful and it is sooo peaceful and perfect here. I love being in your presence. I am in awe of your creativity. How ever do you come up with these beautiful ideas?" she asks with bright and glossy eyes.

"Well, I am the Creator.... you know what else can I say," He states confidently and winks.

The Father and Eve laugh loudly while The Father tends to the garden. Eve wipes the dirt off of her clothes.

"If I wanted to grow a garden like this, what tips could you give me?" she asks. She was totally breath taken.

Eve walks around admiring the garden in awe of its beauty and moves closer to touch the red apple tree in the garden.

"You should always follow the instructions that are written in the owner's manual. If you don't, it can cause problems that you were not expecting….. Don't touch that tree Eve or eat anything from it unless you are ready to die!" The Father's voice raised.

The Father stops tending to the garden and looks at Eve. Eve moves her hand quickly from the plant with a frightened expression.

"Everything that looks good doesn't mean it's good for you," He states gently.

The Father wipes the dirt off of his hands and stands up.

"Yes, Daddy I hear you," she states humbly while looking at her Father with childlike eyes.

Eve stands in front of The Father with her eyes looking towards the ground.

"But, do you understand Me?" The Father asks seriously while softly putting his hands on her cheeks.

Eve embraces The Father tightly and He wraps his loving arms around her.

"Yes! I do, Daddy!" she utters assuredly.

While still embracing The Father, Eve stares at the beautiful garden, and then looks into the direction of the apple tree.

Grocery Store

There are bright red apples on sale, other fruits, and vegetables in the aisle of the produce section. Beautiful naturally grey haired, 81 year old Eve is pushing a cart into the produce section of the grocery store. She has crow's feet around her eyes but few wrinkles which make it difficult to identify her age. While Eve is walking through the fruit aisle she notices the luscious red apples on sale, makes a facial expression of disgust and keeps walking. She sees Bathsheba 21, dressed in hi-cut booty shorts with a half top on revealing her cleavage. She has a ginger brown complexion, shapely body and full lips. Bathsheba is bending down with her butt in the air while looking over her shoulder and sucking a lollipop. Men are staring at Bathsheba with lust in their eyes and the women are rolling and cutting their eyes in condescension.

"Bathsheba is that you? Now girl, you know you need to stop," she says while laughing and shaking her head.

Eve stops rolling her cart in front of the apples for sale and begins to talk to Bathsheba. Bathsheba and Eve hug each other.

"How is that husband of yours doing?" she inquires while looking at Bathsheba with the side eye.

"He is doing fine Mrs. E. He has been deployed more than I would like, but he is doing good."

Bathsheba licks her lollipop as she talks and adjusts her noticeable cleavage in her half top.

"You know you have a good man so why are you going around acting like you ain't married? Now, you know you are better than that," she states with concern as she lightly grips Bathsheba's chin to get her full attention.

"If I can be honest, sometimes I get lonely and I want a man's attention," she voices with sadness.

Bathsheba looks into Eve's, then looks to the ground with her lollipop in her hand.

"Girrlll, well, it looks like you have been successful with all these men gawking at you and licking their lips," she giggles and whispers into Bathsheba's ear.

Eve looks around the grocery store at the men and women's expressions while holding her hand out.

"Do you have a few minutes or are you in a rush? I want to share something with you. Let's grab a bite to eat," she kindly states with a soothing tone.

Eve pushes her cart through the aisles as people continue to stare. "I have nothing but time on my hands," she says boldly while looking at her spectators.

Bathsheba switches while sucking her lollipop. Eve pushes her grocery cart to the cash register and pays for her groceries. Then, Eve and Bathsheba walk in the direction of the eatery on the other side of the grocery store. Bathsheba and Eve find a table and sit down.

"I must've been about your age when Adam began a new job working long hours. In fact, it was his dream job because this role gave him authority and power. He seemed to be extremely happy, but we were separated at times which also made me a little lonely. One day, I went to my father's house to pick up some of his garden vegetables to take to a restaurant that used him as a vendor. I walked into the restaurant to talk to the owner, and I gave her the vegetables from my dad's garden," she stated while pushing up her sleeves.

Chapter 3

Eye Patch Needed

"So if your eye- even your good eye- causes you to lust, gouge it out and throw it away"
-Matthew 5:29 NLV

Gabriella's Restaurant

The dimly lit restaurant is playing live R&B music when Eve enters. The owner, Gabriella, a 30 year old woman has a mocha brown complexion and curvaceous body. She has a welcoming personality and loves Eve like a sister. Gabriella warmly embraces Eve around her neck and helps her put the bags filled with fruits and vegetables on the bar counter. Eve and Gabriela hug tightly.

"How are you doing, Boo? Girl, these vegetables look amazing. Your dad has the best produce ever," she states emotionally with adoration and praise.

Gabriella looks through the bag of produce, pulls out the fruits and vegetables one at a time and then put them back in the bag smiling and dancing.

"I am doing well! You look amazing! I will make sure I tell Daddy that you are impressed with the food that comes from his garden. You know how he loves praise! You know we surely appreciate your business. Wow, things have surely picked up in here and it's not even nighttime yet," she lovingly highlights Gabriella's business accomplishments.

Eve stops speaking as she is mesmerized by the musician singing.

"Earth to Eve, Earth to Eve," Gabriella calls while waving her hand in front of Eve's face.

Eve's eyes are still glued to the musician.

Gabriella's voice raises, "Dang, Eve! Snap out of it!"

"Who is he? It's like he's penning my life with his words," Eve inquisitively asks as she stares at the musician intently.

The musician is staring at Eve across the room.

"So, I guess next you're going to tell me that he is killing you softly. His name is Boa Jones. Here, girl! Drink this water and cool off!" she sarcastically states while poking her lips out to the side.

Gabriella hands Eve a glass of water and shakes her head while she wipes off the bar counter.

"No see, the real question is how is Adam?" she says asks adamantly.

Gabriella stops wiping the counter to look at Eve with one hand on her hip.

"He is doing just fine," she slowly speaks while paying only a quarter of attention to Gabriella.

Eve continuously gazes at Boa while she sips on her water. Boa is a 30 year old man with a sculpted physique. He has a beautiful brown complexion and a contagious smile. Eve claps her hands while standing and staring at the musician in his eyes after he finishes his song.

Adam's Job at Uniquely Designed

Adam is in the office with his boss, Mr. King a gray haired man with broad shoulders whose wearing a tailored business suit. They are sitting in an office with a beautiful view of the city.

"Thank you for taking time out of your busy schedule to meet with me today," he eagerly states.

Adam crosses his legs, opens his notepad, and pays close attention to his boss. Mr.King walks to the corner of his desk, scoots the desk's items over and sits on its edge.

"First, I would like to say that it is my pleasure to meet with you. You remind me so much of myself and you have wonderful potential. I've called you into my office today because I would like to make you the lead on a global project. As you know, I have creative control over every creation and all the work here at Uniquely Designed. I have decided to give you authority to run lead on the U Name It Project. I can't wait to see your creative branding ideas come into fruition. And, yes Adam this is a promotion. You have been here the longer than anyone other than myself, so I wanted to give you this opportunity. This is one of our biggest accounts due its global nature.Therefore, make sure you get the job done in excellence and expeditiously," he smiled while offering Adam a firm handshake.

"I am at a loss for words! Thank you so much! I will do my best and I will not let you down," Adam stands with a huge smile on his face and shakes his boss's hand firmly.

Gabriella's Restaurant

Eve and Gabriella are at the restaurant are at the bar. The musician approaches them, after his performance

"Thanks for the opportunity to sing at your wonderful establishment," he says smoothly, pulls out a bar stool and sits closely to Eve.

"You are a talented musician indeed," she says seriously.

Eve puts her hands on her hips as she speaks directly to Boa.

"Thanks again! Who is this beautiful creation of perfection standing here with you?" he asks flirtatiously.

Eve gulps her drink as she turns around clearly smitten.

"This is Eve. A happily married dear friend of mine. Don't even try it over here, Boa," she roared protectively.

Gabriella still has her hands on her hips as she speaks emphatically to Boa.

"Hello! I am happy to make your acquaintance," she responded timidly while bashfully staring at Boa.

Boa and Eve shake hands with a noticeable attraction to one another.

Adam's Job at Uniquely Designed

"With you as the firm's first corporate leader, I'm assigning a young lady to work with you, who will study and document your moral behaviors and ethical business practices in efforts to benefit the good of everyone," Mr. King states like a proud father.

The Boss calls up to the front desk and asks for the receptionist to allow Taipan, 25 a year old, pecan complexioned woman, to come to his office. Taipan enters the office wearing a tightly fitted red dress that hugs her voluptuous body in the right places. She stares at Adam intently with a twinkle in her eye. Adam is physically attracted to Taipan the moment she walks through the door.

"It's nice to meet you Adam. I have heard a lot about you and it will be an honor to study and examine your professional practices," she says seductively while running her fingers through her hair.

"It's my pleasure to meet you," he says quickly and turns his head toward his boss with his eyes wide open.

He adjusts his tie and clears his throat before he speaks.

"Well, my job is done here. Get to work," Mr. King enthusiastically commands with a grin.

"Thanks again for the opportunity! I won't let you down," Adam affirms.

Adam smiles and shakes the Boss's hand, and leaves the office. Adam and Taipan walk out of the Boss's office without saying much to each other. Taipan walks in front Adam while he intently fights to not look at Taipan's sculpted peach shaped behind. Taipan grins as she catwalks down the hall into Adam's office.

"Have a seat," he says without smiling.

Adam holds out his hand and sits down himself. Taipan sits down and picks up a picture of Adam and Eve that was sitting on Adam's desk.

"Who is this gorgeous woman, if I may ask?" she nosily inquires.

"It's my wife, Eve," he states sternly looking directly in Taipan's eyes.

Gabriella's Restaurant

"Eve you are absolutely stunning. Can I buy you ladies lunch?" Boa asks admiring Eve.

Boa stares captivated by Eve's beauty.

"Boa, now you know if I own the restaurant why would you have to buy me lunch? That doesn't make any sense," Gabriella states frustrated and well aware of his tactics.

She walks into the kitchen and leaves Eve and Boa at the bar.

"Well, I should be going but it was nice to meet you," Eve says chewing on the ice from her glass.

Boa grabs Eve's hand and stares deeply into her eyes.

"You should stay," he insists. Boa pulls out the chair next to him wishing that Eve would sit down next to him. Eve sits down. Gabriella looks out the kitchen to see what is happening.

"Now that's more like it. So, tell me Eve where are you from?" he inquisitively grins showing his pearly white teeth.

"I am a D.C. native. I was born and raised here. Been here all my life. How about you? Where are you from?" she inquires while taking a sip of her drink.

"I am from up North but I came here for change of scenery, better opportunities and to meet new people like you. Would you mind showing me around the city if it's not too much to ask? Before you answer please understand, you will just be a friendly guide for me. Our outings will be strictly innocent," he asks hopefully as he puts his hand in prayer posture.

"I will give it some thought and get back to you," Eve hesitantly responds while fidgeting.

Gabriella comes out of the kitchen and interrupts their conversation.

"The kitchen is closed. We reopen at 5:00 p.m. So, I guess there won't be any lunch today," she raises her voice with an intensely fevered stare.

"Well, I should be going! I have a hair appointment It's getting late! Thanks for lunch," she laughs and gulps the remainder of her drink.

"You don't even look like you need your hair done. You look simply gorgeous as you are," he compliments.

Eve stands speechless as she smiles and rubs her hair.

"Let's make a deal, if you show me around the city I will take you to lunch or dinner. It's your choice," Boa whispers leaning in Eve's direction.

Eve smiles and Gabriella interrupts Eve and Boa's conversation.

"Eve can I have a word with you in the kitchen please?" she interrupts with her squinted eyes.

Eve rolls her eyes and walks into the kitchen behind Gabriella.

"Eve what are you doing? You know you have a man that loves and adores you at home. You are his rib. So what are you really doing?" she asks out of concern.

Gabriella grabs Eve's shoulders and looks into her eyes.

"You know... Adam is always working and I get lonely sometimes," Eve's voice breaks as she speaks.

Eve's Marital Reflection

"I go out of my way to make his favorite meals. I wear sexy clothes, and I make sure that I look good for my man," she tearfully voices while wiping her eyes.

Joe's *All the Things* plays in the background. Eve places Adam's favorite meals on the candle lit table. She is wearing sexy lingerie and is flaunting a new hairdo and makeup. Adam arrives at their modern styled home extremely late from work and is having trouble taking off his tie. Eve greets him at the door with a juicy kiss.

"Hey, Honey! Let me get that for you" she says and caters to Adam taking his briefcase from his hand.

Eve puts the briefcase on the floor near the door. Then, she helps her husband remove his tie.

"Work has been hectic because we have several new creative projects. Also, your husband, yes your husband has been promoted as the lead on the You Name It Project. This is a huge deal! It is my job as VP of Brand Marketing to name the new creations for this global project. My boss aka upper management, has given me the authority and the power to establish names for brands that will appeal to the global masses. This is a huge opportunity for me to show my boss what I can do. Then, after work I went out to eat with my coworkers and now I am going straight to bed. Love you!" Adam states excitedly but in an exhausted tone.

"Congratulations! I am proud of you! But I made your favorite meal... curried potatoes with coconut rice and mixed greens!" she yelled frustratedly as Adam went up to their bedroom.

"Pack some for my lunch tomorrow and I will eat it then. Now, let me get some sleep because I have a long day to tomorrow," he replied inconsiderately and continued to their bedroom.

Gabriella's Restaurant

"He is so consumed with work and climbing the corporate ladder that it seems like he barely recognizes me. I feel like I am doing this thing called life without him. So, when you ask me about what I am doing.... No disrespect, but you don't know my story," she says with tears streaming down her face.

Eve puts her hands up in frustration and walks out of the kitchen.

"I thought you forgot about me. Here's my card. I really look forward to hearing from you soon," he said seductively looking at Eve like a snack.

Eve smiles, takes the card, and looks at Gabriella from the corner of her eyes. Gabriella has her hand on her hip and shakes her head.

"It was nice seeing you and make sure you tell your husband, yes I said your husband Adam that I said hello," she says sternly stressing the husband portion.

Eve waves her hand and walks out of the restaurant. Boa takes a look at Eve's butt as she walks away.

"Goodnight, Eve," Boa says in a silky smooth tone with a huge grin on his face.

Boa lifts up his glass and does an air toast. Gabriella looks at Boa and rolls her eyes.

Joe's song *All the Things* stops playing.

Chapter 4

Killing Me Softly

"But each person is tempted when he is lured and enticed by his own desire" -James 1:14 ESV

Adam and Eve's Home

Adam and Eve are lying in bed with the sheets covering their bodies.

"Good night," Adam said yawning and closing his eyes.

Adam turned over in the bed and pulled all of the covers off of Eve.

"Goodnight," she said softly with tears in her eyes.

Eve shakes her head in dismay. She goes to the bathroom looks at herself in the mirror and touches her hair. She begins to contemplate Boa's compliments. She looks in her coat pocket, finds the card Boa gave her and considers calling him. The next morning, she hands Adam a cup of lemon water, his lunch and a piece of guacamole toast topped with boiled eggs for breakfast.

"Thank you," he said while rushing out the door.

Eve goes upstairs and looks in the mirror wondering if something is wrong with her. She picks up Boa's card and calls him from her cell phone. He answered after the third ring just before she was going to hang up.

"Hello," he answered in a deep alluring tone.

"Hi, Boa. This is Eve. I was calling to see if you had any plans today and if you were still up for touring of the city?" she asked nervously while biting her nails.

"Of course, I am available around twelve today. How does that work for you?" he asked with a grin you could hear over the phone.

"Twelve works perfectly. Where would you like to meet? I can pick you up if you like," she offered kindly.

Boa interrupts quickly.

"No, no that's not a good idea. I can pick you up or we can meet next door to Gabriella's at the coffee shop," he advised confidently.

"Ok. Let's meet at the coffee shop. See you soon," she smiled ear to ear.

"See you soon, Beautiful," he said in a charming voice.

Eve hung up the phone, smiled, looked at herself in the mirror turning from front to back and then began to dance around.

African American Museum

Eve arrives at the coffee shop before Boa. She sits down and begins to scroll through her phone. She lifts her head up and notices Boa standing over her with a dozen beautiful purple roses.

"Thank you so much Boa. These roses are so beautiful. You shouldn't have," Eve smiles while smelling the roses.

"It was my pleasure! Beautiful roses for a beautiful lady," Boa says gazing into Eve's beautiful brown eyes.

He stares at Eve intently as though he were looking through her soul.

"Well, I guess we should get going," Eve insists to break Boa's alluring gaze.

Music is playing while Eve and Boa walk around touring prominent figures at the African American Museum.

"Wow, time sure flies! It's almost 4:00 p.m., and we still haven't seen the most modern floor highlighting Oprah Winfrey's accomplishments. We come back again and continue our tour when you are available. Now, are you up for a bite to eat?" Eve asks as she pulls Boa's arm to walk in the direction of the museum's exit.

Boa follows Eve as she continues to guide him around the city.

I know just the place where we can go to eat. You can't say you have had a tour of D.C. without visiting Ben's Chili Bowl. Their food is really good and they have vegetarian options as well," Eve suggests to Boa as she walks with her hand tucked in his.

"Okay, let's check it out. I am game. It sounds good," he says while rubbing his tummy.

"You ain't said nothing but a word," Eve smiles as she leads the ways to Ben's.

Ben's Chili Bowl

They arrive at Ben's Chili Bowl around 6:00 p.m. and walk up to the counter to order their food..

"So, what's good on their menu?" he asks while looking over his shoulder nervously.

"I hear the half smoke with everything on it is good. I have been vegan since the beginning of my time, sooo I am just getting the vegan chili. It's really tasty," she replies.

Boa talks to the cashier who is waiting to take his order.

"Can I have two half smokes with everything on it and a vegan chili please with two bottles of water?" he asks flashing his Orbitz white teeth.

"You sure can and your order will be ready in less than 10 minutes," the female cashier flirtatiously grins and switches away.

Boa and Eve pick up their order and find a table in the back of Ben's Chili Bowl. They begin to eat their taste bud satisfying meal with little conversation.

"Now, this right here is the best half smoke I have had in my life. You need to taste this, Eve. A little meat never hurt anybody," he tempts seductively in a fake Caribbean accent.

Eve is tickled and is at a loss for words. So, she stuffs her mouth with a big spoonful of her vegan chili and then wipes one corner of her mouth with a napkin.

"Now that's a misconception…granted, just because it looks real good doesn't mean that it's good for you."

Boa licks his lips and leans in closer to Eve from across their table. He uses his napkin to wipe the other corner of Eve's mouth.

"Sooo Eve, are you talking about me or the half smoke?" he asks without apprehension still leaning into Eve's personal space.

Boa locks eyes with Eve. Then, a young curvaceous, lady comes out of the restroom and notices Boa. Boa recognizes her, lowers his head and puts his hand up on the side of his head to avoid conversation.

"Boa, Boa is that you? How are you? Did you know our high school reunion is coming up?" Indigo asks energetically while wiping her hands with a towel.

Boa acts as though he doesn't want to engage in the conversation and gives Indigo a very short answer.

"Yeah, I am good," he says without giving her any eye contact.

"Well, it was nice seeing you. Gooo Ballou Knights!" she cheers excitedly.

Boa waved and continued to eat his food.

"That is truly a coincidence. She went to your high school in New York and you bumped into each other at the Ben' s Chili Bowl. Inquiring minds would like to know if she thinks the half smokes are good," Eve retorts sarcastically as she continues to eat her chili.

"Oh, so you do stand-up comedy on the side?" Boa diverts and laughs.

They both laugh while continuing to enjoy their meal.

"I truly enjoyed my time with you today," Boa admits while putting their trash in the trash can.

"Likewise, I enjoyed myself as well! Today, was a bit different for me, because I have only been out with my husband," Eve contemplates her actions somewhat remorsefully.

"Can we meet tomorrow? I would like to take you to a special secret place," Boa asks in a gentleman like manner while putting on his coat.

"I don't know. I don't want to make a habit of our outings because I am married you know. Sooo, do you have a special lady in your life? Do you have any children? I want to learn more about you. Tell me about yourself," she says while wrapping her scarf around her neck joyfully.

"No, I don't have a special lady in my life nor do I have any kids. I just want to repay you for your kindness to me. We can meet here around 11:00 a.m., because I want another half smoke. These half smokes are on point," he says while rubbing his hands together.

"Ok, I will go with you tomorrow. We can meet here at 11:00 a.m.," Eve smiles as she slowly gives into her temptation.

They stare into each other's eyes. Eve breaks eye contact purposely. They leave the restaurant; and as they said their goodbyes they affectionately hug and slightly kiss, but Eve stops instantly.

"I am sorry. I just can't do this," Eve cries because of her adulterous actions.

Boa attempts to comfort Eve, but she walks away highly disappointed with her behavior.

"Eve, Eve!" Boa yells desiring to comfort Eve, as he looks at her voluptuous behind.

Eve continues to walk to her car without responding to Boa. Boa watches Eve walk away while thinking about her thick thighs.

Chapter 5

Don't Sleep On It

"Watch and pray that you may not enter into temptation" -Matthew 26:41 ESV

Adam and Eve's House

Eve is in bed sleep wearing sweatpants and an oversized t-shirt. Adam enters the house with roses and notices the roses in a vase that Boa had given her. He was unaware that another man had given her flowers. Adam goes into the kitchen expecting dinner to be made but his expectation is not met. Adam takes a shower and hops in bed with Eve. Adam attempts to cuddle with his wife, but she pushes his hands and body away from her. Adam and Eve go to sleep without praying together. The next morning, Eve is dressed earlier than usual wearing an fragrance that's unfamiliar to Adam. She is wearing a dress that highlights her figure a little more than normal and a new hair style that is actually from two days ago. Adam sees his wife in a new light.

"Good morning, Evie! Baby, you look absolutely stunning. You are wearing a new fragrance. I am not sure I like the smell of it though, and I see you went to the hairdresser yesterday," Adam says hugging Eve tightly from behind as they look in the mirror together.

"No, I had my hair done the day you came home with your big news after your feast with your coworkers ," Eve explained to Adam calmly wearing a huge smile.

Eve continues to look at herself in the mirror unbothered and joyfully while she thought about Boa's compliments.

"Well, let me run! I hope you enjoy this beautiful day," Eve says exuberantly grabbing her purse and walking in the direction of the door.

"What are your plans today? Why are you leaving so early?" Adam asks while getting a taste of his own medicine.

"You know I have to be about my Father's business," Eve says while opening the door.

"Tell Dad I said thanks for making you for me! Have a great day, sweetheart," Adam gratefully expresses with a worried look on his face.

"I will and you do the same," she states as she walks out of the door.

Eve's Father's Garden

Eve's Father is working in the garden.

"Good morning, Daddy!" Eve says with a huge smile on her face.

"Good morning, my daughter! What are you doing up so early?" he asks as he looks up at Eve suspiciously with one raised eyebrow.

The father stands up and digs the shovel in the ground leaning on it. He gives Eve his undivided attention, waiting to hear her voice.

"I wanted to help you by dropping off the fruits and vegetables to Gabriella for the Taste of D.C. before time got away from me. This a great opportunity for you to showcase the produce of your garden to the world. Daddy, I don't think they are ready for what you are offering. They will taste and see that it is good! Yessss! This is a major accomplishment that will open doors for the next generations," Eve praised her father and his work confidently.

"Ummhmm. How is Adam?" The Father interjected with a stern look on his face.

"He is doing well. He told me to tell you hello and to thank you for making me for him," she repeated Adam's message without fail while looking at that beautiful apple tree.

They both laugh and the Father hands Eve the fruits and vegetables.

"Well tell Adam that it was my pleasure. Eve, is that a new fragrance that you are wearing? It's unusual. It's not like the fragrance that you normally wear. I love the other fragrance you wear so much better," he shares freely as he sniffs with a stank look on his face.

"Adam said the same thing. Hmmm! Daddy, does it smell that bad?" Eve questions as she sniffs her shirt.

"I wouldn't say that, but I like the other fragrance you wear much better. It smells fresh and pure," the Father honestly commented while pulling his shirt over his nose.

"Well, I must admit these fruits and vegetable look so good. You have outdone yourself again," Eve sings with a bright smile as she places the fruits and vegetables into a crate.

"Thanks, Sweetheart! Now, Eve please remember that what looks good does not always mean that it is good for you. FYI, I am not talking about the fruits and vegetables," the Father said as He winked his eye and waved away the funk of Eve's fragrance.

"I hear you, Daddy," she says timidly in a soft voice as she picks up the crate.

"Please, make sure that you hear and understand Me," the Father said adamantly while pointing his finger directly at Eve.

"I love you and OK, Daddy!" she confirmed that she understood exactly what her Father was telling her.

"Remember, you are the first born of my daughters and I love you very much!" The Father emphasized with a tear in his eye.

The Father and Eve exchange their goodbyes. Boa calls Eve from his old 90's cell phone, and she decides to meet him at Ben's Chili Bowl, forgetting to drop off the fruits and vegetables to Gabriella. Eve walks into Ben's Chili Bowl. Then she walks towards the area where Boa is sitting. Boa gets up from his seat when he notices Eve and pulls out her chair.

"Out of Zion, the perfection of beauty, God hath shined," Boa recites making Eve feel like she is the only woman in the room.

"Psalm 50:2, wow impressive," she commends him for his biblical knowledge and becomes even more attracted to him.

"I grew up in church, and I was the minister of music," he reminisces about the good ol' days.

"You have such a lovely voice. What made you stop ministering music?" Eve inquires and is determined to get to know him better.

"Well, it's a rather complicated story. Let me see, you know some people just get jealous of your talent and things just didn't work out with me and the guy in charge. So, I just left the church. The whole situation just left a bad burnt taste in my mouth, so I just stopped singing gospel music all together. I decided to do my own thing and now I have a huge following.

"I am so sorry to hear that. I wish that never happened to you, because you're such a nice guy. It seems like you have a good heart," Eve confesses in a heartfelt manner while gently touching Boa's face.

"Well, I am misunderstood quite often. I hope you don't mind that I took the liberty of ordering for us. This half smoke is so delicious. Eve, you have to take just a small bite of this. It's not going to hurt you. Please just take a little bite for me. Pretty please," he begged with his lip poked out and with praying hands.

Boa continues to eat and enjoy his meal.

"Boa, is it that good? You make it look so good by the way you're eating it. Well, I guess a little bite won't hurt me," she accepts his offer and opens her mouth wide.

Boa feeds Eve a piece of his half smoke while looking into her soul. Eve closes her eyes and enjoys the delicious taste of Ben's Chili Bowl's famous loaded half smoke.

Then, Eve opens her eyes and smiles. Boa wipes the leftover chili from the corner of Eve's mouth off with his finger and then licks the chili from his finger. They both stare intently into each other eyes speechlessly.

"Eve, can I please take you to that special place now?" Boa seductively asks and smirks with puppy eyes.

Without hesitation, Eve stands up out of her seat, and Boa stands up quickly as well. They eagerly walk out of the restaurant.

"Eve, what is that aromatic fragrance you are wearing? I absolutely love the way it smells. I like it even better than the fragrance that you wore the first day I met you," Eve smiles with all teeth as she falls romantically for Boa.

As Eve walks ahead, she looks back at Boa over her shoulder and says, "A woman never tells."

Eve flips her hair and continues to strut like a runway model. Boa can hardly contain his intensely lustful desire for Eve. As they are walking, a woman approaches Boa and taps him on his shoulder.

"Hey, Boa! How are you and why haven't you returned my calls?" she asks with an attitude and folded hands with her body weight shifted to one side.

"I am good and it was nice seeing you again. I will call you soon," Boa concluded the conversation quickly, because he was totally focused on Eve.

Boa concludes, walks out of the restaurant and catches up with Eve.

"You sure do know a lot of people being that you just moved here from New York," Eve points out as she continues to strut down U Street.

"I admit that I do. It's because of this ol' music thang. Now, I did tell you that I have a lot of followers. Now, the special place I am taking you is to the studio. I hope that's ok with you," Boa asks and smiles holding out his hands.

Eve nods and they walk to their destination.

Chapter 6

Oops, I Bumped My Head

"Then desire when it has conceived gives birth to sin," -James 1:15 ESV

Studio Apartment

They arrive at the studio apartment with a piano in the middle of the floor, studio equipment and a couch.

"Ta dah! Here we are! Make yourself comfortable! I have been working on this new song which is inspired by you and I want you to hear it," Boa says staring at Eve and holding her hands.

Eve walks around the apartment and takes a seat on the couch. Boa begins to take off his coat and unbutton his shirt. Eve is mesmerized by his sculpted chest.

"I just need to get a little more comfortable. Do you want something to drink? I make a mean apple martini," Boa says while making his chest bounce up and down.

"I will pass. I don't drink alcohol. Do you have any bottled water?" she asks clearing her throat and the filthy thoughts from her mind.

"No, I don't have any bottles of water but please try this apple martini. It so good, and you can't even taste the alcohol. It's not going to hurt you and will even help you to loosen up some," Boa says convincingly and pours Eve a drink.

Boa looks Eve in her eyes which encourages her to take a sip of the apple martini. Eve continues to sip on her martini slowly, until it is almost gone. Boa begins to play a seductive song that touches Eve's heart stirring her emotions. By this time, Boa has taken his shirt off completely. Just then, the doorbell rings. It is the beautiful women who Eve and Boa had seen the first night at Ben's Chili Bowl.

"Hey, Indigo! What took you so long to get here?" Boa questions as she walks through the door.

Indigo runs her fingers down his chest and then they kiss intimately. Eve looks at them and gulps the rest of her drink. On one hand Eve is curious about what she is witnessing and on the other hand she is turned on by their intimacy.

"Let me introduce you to Eve. Eve this is Indigo, Indigo this is Eve," Boa presents by graciously moving his hand in their direction.

Indigo and Eve say hello to each other. Indigo touches Eve's hair and skin.

"You are sooo beautiful and your skin is so soft. You look so familiar to me but, I can't put my finger on it," she states staring into Eve's eyes.

"Thank you! You are gorgeous yourself. I believe you remember seeing me at Ben's Chili Bowl," Eve replies timidly with a quivering voice and heart beating into overdrive.

"Mmmhmm," she mumbles with a smirk on her face.

Boa gazes at the women as they are converse holding a bottle of Moët in one hand and a glass in his other hand.

"I think we should get a little more acquainted," he says in an inviting manner.

The three of them sit on the bed and Boa and Indigo begin to make out. Eve watches in awe and is aroused by Boa and Indigo's foreplay. Boa begins to kiss Eve all over her body and she attempts to resist him but cannot.

"Stop! No… I can't," she states but gives into the temptation slowly.

"You know you want it and it's going to be really good. It's not going to harm you. You'll love it," Boa insists kissing Eve all over her body.

"Oh, she's a first timer. Relax, Eve and enjoy the ride. This experience will change your entire life. Trust me. You'll see," Indigo persuades while she watches.

Boa pulls the sheets over his head, covers Eve's entire body and makes more passionate advances. Eve gives into the burning flames of her desires as Indigo joins the party. Once the intimate session has concluded, Eve realizes she has never been more satisfied.

She checks the time and sees it is 9:00p.m. "I truly enjoyed myself, but I have to go. Oh, my God," she admits frantically scrambling to put on her clothes.

"Here's my number! Call me," Indigo insists with a smile on her face.

"Ok," Eve smiles as she looks for her keys in her purse.

Eve and Indigo smile at each other and Eve rushes out the door.

Eve runs to her car. She looks at her cell phone and has missed several calls from Gabriella, Adam and her Father. Eve turns around and notices the fruits and vegetables that she was supposed to drop off for her Father to Gabriella still in the back seat of her car. Furious with herself and remorseful, Eve begins banging her head and intensely grabs the stirring wheel of the car.

Chapter 7

My Guilty Pleasure

..."and sin when it is fully grown brings forth death." -James 1:15 ESV

Gabriella's Restaurant

Eve finally meets up with Gabrielle to deliver her Father's produce.

Gabriella asks, "Where have you been? I have been worried sick about you? Adam and your Father have been calling me like crazy!" she exclaims.

Gabriella looks at Eve, shakes her head and puts her head down. She begins to hug Eve.

Gabriella asks, "Are you ok? What is that awful fragrance you are wearing?" she asked while holding her nose.

Eve says, "I am ok. I guess you don't like it either," and begins to cry.

Adam and Eve's House

Adam is sitting in the family room waiting for Eve to return home. When she enters the house Adam jumps out of his seat.

"Where have you been? I have been trying to get in contact with you all day long. What is that smell? Adam asks in a worried manner.

Eve rolls her eyes.

"Adam, I am surprised you are not at work or out with your coworkers. I have been out and I don't have time for this conversation. I am going to bed," Eve frustratedly responds as she walks up the stairs to their bedroom.

"Come on, Baby, you know I have been working a lot of long hours to impress my boss. I really want him to know that he made the right decision entrusting me with this account. This is a great opportunity for rewards and bonuses if things go well. So, please don't be upset with me, I will do better," he pours out his heart sincerely to Eve.

"Save it, Adam! This has been going on long enough. I am tired, I am about to take a shower, and then I am going to straight to sleep," she says with a look of disgust on her face.

While Adam is in the bed researching information for work, Eve takes her shower. She begins to reminisce about her exotic evening while Adam thinks about Taipan's curvaceous body and beautiful eyes.

"Come on Evie Eve, I thought we could spend some time together tonight. You know a brother has needs and it's been a long time," Adam begs while air grinding.

"And, this woman has needs too, the need for this conversation to end and the need for you to leave me alone. Good night, Adam! I am going to sleep now," Eve states adamantly as she fluffs up her pillow and lays her head down.

Eve quickly pulls the covers from over her body that she was sharing with Adam, and they lay in bed with their backs towards each other. Adam wraps his arms around his own body lying in a fetal position and with a look of dejection. The next morning, Adam leaves for work while Eve is preparing her breakfast when the phone rings.

"Hello," she pleasantly greets as she spreads jam on her toast.

"Good morning, Eve! This is Indigo! How are you and what are you doing today?" she asks as she enters the building.

She smiles, strokes her hair, and says, "Hey, Indigo. I don't have any plans. I was going to spend some time with my Father, but I can cancel those plans. What are you doing today?"

"I don't have much to do today except run by my office for a few hours, and then I was wondering if you would like to get together. I wanna take you somewhere today. I can come and pick you up if that's all right," Indigo offers warmly as she waits for an elevator.

"Sure, that sounds perfect. My address is 760 Millers Avenue, Suitland, MD. What time should I be ready?" she asked enthusiastically putting the jam in the refrigerator.

"I will pick you up around 12:00 p.m.," she answers ands walks into the elevator.

"Ok, I will see you then." Eve smiles and hangs up the phone.

Adam's Job at Uniquely Designed

Taipan knocks on Adam's office door and he motions for her to enter. Taipan stares at the picture of Adam and Eve on Adam's desk and smirks.

So, how long have you and your wife been married?" she questions with her legs crossed with her fist on her chin.

"We have been married for about seven years, but I don't like to talk about my marriage in the workplace," he authoritatively states intentionally not looking in her direction.

"I can respect that," she replied looking intently into his eyes while licking her lips.

Adam quickly switches the subject and cleared his throat.

"Have you researched the names I emailed you with the trademark division to make sure they are not currently in use?" he diverted.

"Yes, I have and all of the names are free and clear to use. Is there anything else you would like me to do for you today before I leave?" she proposes in a sexy voice.

"No thank you, Taipan, you are free to leave for the day," Adam said with his eyes fixed at the papers on his desk.

Taipan walks towards the door of Adam's office but before exiting she seductively bends down to grab her briefcase with her sculpted behind directed to and caught by Adam's gaze. She looks over her shoulder, slowly stands and grins at Adam. He begins to blush, then puts his hand on his forehead looking back down at the work on his desk. Taipan waves and chuckles as she leaves the office.

Adam and Eve's House

The doorbell rings, and Eve answers the door for Indigo.

"Hey, girl! Come on in and have a seat. I'll be ready in a few minutes," Eve exclaims while rushing into her room.

"Take your time. I'm in no rush! You have the perfect home," she compliments as she walks around admiring the beautiful décor.

Eve comes back to the room and notices that Indigo staring at a picture of Eve and her husband.

"OK, I am ready. So where are we going?" Eve asks and puts on her shoes.

"I will tell you in the car. I know you will truly enjoy yourself. Eve, you are so beautiful and you look great," Indigo emphasized with a big smile.

"Wow, thank you! We women need to hear that from time to time," Eve states sadly with her eyes to the ground.

Eve and Indigo's Outing

Indigo and Eve walk to the car and began their drive.

"Honestly, how did you enjoy yesterday's extravaganza?" Indigo inquires while looking back and forth at the road and Eve.

"It was truly fulfilling not like anything I have experienced before. My husband and I are each other's only lovers. So yesterday's experience was simply exhilarating. My husband and I have never practiced pleasure in such a way. It makes me think about the line in Harlem nights when the cop wants to leave his family for Sunshine. He calls and his kid answers the phone. He says put your mom on the phone. Then, he says to his wife, 'Honey I'm not coming back home anymore'," Eve laughs as she gives her example.

Indigo laughs as she listens to Eve speak.

"So, if you thought yesterday was something what I am about to introduce you to will blow your mind," Indigo assures as she turns into the parking lot.

"Sounds interesting! Please enlighten me," Eve curiously expresses as she gets out of the car.

Eve and Indigo enter a building and walk to the end of the hallway. Indigo knocks on a door five times slowly and it opens allowing the ladies to enter. In the room, there are men and women in a line waiting to have STD laboratory tests and physicals performed. Eve curiously looks around wondering what Indigo has up her sleeve.

"Eve, I know you are wondering what we are doing. Let me explain. I would like for you to become a part of a secret group called SES. I have been a member for about two years now and have never had a dull moment. The members of this group indulge in ecstasy adventures. New members of the group fill out paperwork that describe their erotic interests. The organizers of SES want to know your likes, your dislikes, your fantasies, dreams, and intimate desires. All of the members have aliases. We do not share real names, marital status, where we live or our occupations. For added spice, we dress the part of our fantasies. I literally have had some of the best times being a part of this group. When you meet the SES members, I think you will be swayed to join. Eve, does it sound like something in which you might be interested?" Indigo asks eagerly with both her hands held out and her head tilted to the side.

"Wow! What does the acronym SES stand for?" Eve questions while looking at her surroundings.

Indigo pulls out an SES marketing card.

"SES stands for Spontaneous Exhibitionists Sex. Trust me! You can start your escapades as soon as your test results come back. You will absolutely love it!" Indigo confidently states giving Eve the application.

Eve sees some of the attractive people who are apart of this secret group. She fills out the paperwork and has her STD labs performed.

Adam and Eve's House

Adam and Eve are in the bed with their backs towards each other but emotions far apart. They both ponder the activities that have taken place over the last couple of weeks.

"Goodnight, Eve," Adam states with discouragement while shedding a tear.

"Goodnight, Adam," she snaps.

Chapter 8

Run Joe

"Flee from sexual immorality" -1 Corinthians 6:18

Early the next morning around 3:00 a.m. while Eve is still sleeping, Adam calls his father.

"Hey, Son! Why are you up so late? You should be resting. It's been a while since we have talked," he states as though he is wide awake when most people are sleep.

"I know and it's my fault," he somberly admits while wiping his tears.

"What's troubling you? I know something is bothering you because you never call at this hour," the father voices with care.

"It's Eve! Something is truly going on with her and I don't know what it is. She barely talks to me and seems extremely angry. She's beginning to dress with less clothes and isn't giving me the time of day. If I attempt to touch her she moves away from me aggressively. Now, I know I have been investing a lot of time at work, but I don't deserve this," Adam cries seeking resolution.

"Do you still pray together? Have you prayed or read the Bible? Adam, it sounds like you are experiencing spiritual warfare and that you need to fight for your wife right now. She needs you to fight for her! The last time I saw her it seemed like she was going through something, but she did not discuss it with me. I haven't spoken to her in a while, but I can tell she has not been herself lately. Your job as a husband is to be the head of your wife. This is very crucial because what you do has a trickling down effect on the family. Your job is to make sure that you sanctify and cleanse your wife with the washing of water by the word. If you are honest with yourself and think about your actions - What have you not done but were supposed to do in your marriage? Son, you are to present her without having a spot or wrinkle or any such thing that she may be holy and without blemish. Now, don't you work out or go to the gym to make sure that you take care of your body? You are supposed to love Eve like you love yourself and take care of her spiritually, mentally, and physically. You are seeing, tasting, hearing, smelling, and feeling the fruit that you have produced. I am warning you to get your priorities straight and to cover your wife or the results will be devastating," he gently and lovingly guides.

"You are absolutely right and telling nothing but the truth! Thank you, thank you so much! I don't know what I would do without you!" Adam exclaims from his heart.

"You know that I am always here for you no matter the time or hour. Just remember, that our choices have consequences either for good or for bad. Remember this conversation, I will check up on the both of you soon. I love you, son. Now, go get some rest," he kindly asserts.

"Goodnight! I love you too," Adam responds as he wipes tears from his eyes.

The next morning while Eve is in the shower, Adam makes Eve's favorite breakfast. Eve walks downstairs in a tight fitted red dress that he has never seen before.

"Honey, I made your favorite breakfast and I'm really sorry for the times I have neglected you. I apologize for putting my work before you. I promise I will make it up to you. I will do whatever you want me to as long as I can have my Evie Eve back," Adam apologizes as he hands Eve a plate of food.

"I am not eating that right now. But, you can put it in the refrigerator, and I will eat it later," Eve states without even looking at the breakfast as she hands the plate back to Adam.

"Before you leave can we pray together?" Adam asks politely with a tear running down his cheek.

"Adam you are a trip! You have not been interested in praying with me or spending time with me but all of a sudden now you want to pray. Pray, I am listening," Eve asserts agitatedly shaking her head and holding both of her hands out.

Adam grabs Eve's hands and rubs them gently.

"God please bless my marriage! I am so sorry for the way I have treated my wife. Please allow her to love me again. In Jesus name I pray. Amen! Eve, I really wanna just make you happy! I will do anything for you. What can I do to make you love me again?" Adam asks desperately while gripping Eve's hands.

"Adam, I will see you later this evening," she states pulling her hands away and rushes out the door.

Adam's Job at Uniquely Designed

Adam's Boss calls Adam and Taipan into his office.

"I called both of you into my office to tell you what an excellent job you're doing on the You Name It Project. Adam, I knew that you were the man for this job and you have exceeded my expectations! Not only has the project received rave reviews and is trending, but the company wants to give us all of their global projects! You and Taipan have done a wonderful job! You make quite the team! You will definitely receive a promotion with a huge pay raise! Take the rest of the day off! You deserve it," the boss declares proudly shaking Adam and Taipan's hands.

"Thank you, so much! Wow!" Adam says with a smile as he shakes his Boss' hand.

"Thank you this is such an honor," Taipan states with a smile and a twinkle in her eyes.

Adam and Taipan walk into Adam's office and close the door. Adam picks up the phone to call Eve. Taipan takes the phone from Adam's ear slowly hanging up the call. She moves her face closely to Adam's, strokes Adam's face and kisses him.

Adam resists and stops mid kiss." I can't do this! I am married," Adam whimpers as he gently pushes Taipan off of him.

"Then, let me do it," she states while kissing Adam and putting the picture of Adam and his wife face down.

Adam gives in to his temptation.

Gabriella's Restaurant

Eve walks into Gabriella's Restaurant hearing the smooth sound of Boa's voice on the mic. Eve walks back to her usual spot at the bar and listens to Boa sing. She orders a drink from the bartender. Gabriella greets Eve with a warm hug when she notices her.

"Look at you! You are wearing that dress. I know when Adam sees you he is going to lose his mind. You look gorgeous!" she smiles staring at Eve.

Eve twirls around for Gabriella so she can get a better look at her outfit.

"Thank you! He has already seen it," she says quickly and sucks on her straw turning into Boa's direction.

Uuuuhmmmm! What has gotten into you? Something is not right! What is going on with you?" she asks with a concerned look.

"I am just being free and living my best life," Eve answers while smiling at Boa and rolling her neck.

Boa walks up to Eve and gives her a long, intimate hug while Eve closes her eyes, bites her lip and smiles.

"Eve, you look so beautiful on the outside but I don't know what's going on with you on the inside. You are not acting like my Eve and you know the word. It says just as the church is subject to Christ, so let the wife be to her own husband in everything. Come on Eve! You know better than this!" Gabriella shrieks with her hand on her hip.

"Eve defiantly holds up her hand, grabs Boa's hand and declares in a sassy manner, "Ain't nobody got time for that."

Eve and Boa walk out of the restaurant with Eve leading the way. Gabriella shakes her head and looks in disbelief and concern that Eve would say and do such a thing. Eve's phone rings as she is walking out of the restaurant. Adam is calling to tell her about his promotion.

"Congratulations, Adam! It seems like your hard work has paid off and you've gotten everything you wanted," she replies looking at Boa like he is a plate of chicken and waffles.

"Thank you! We should celebrate, tonight! We can do anything you like! I really want to make it up to you for the way that I have been acting recently," he remorsefully laments and leans back in his office chair.

"Hmmm! So, do you really mean anything?" she contemplates as she gazes at Boa.

"Yesss, anything for my beautiful wife," he smiles from the inside out.

"Ok, sounds good. Let's meet at home around 8:30 p.m.," she grins with one eyebrow up.

"8:30, it is," he agrees and ends the call.

Chapter 9

What In The Hell

"Then the eyes of both of them were opened, and they knew they were naked" -Genesis 3:7

Adam and Eve's House

Later that night, Eve creates a candlelight setting in the house with smooth sounds of R&B playing loudly. Adam is amazed that his wife would go to so much trouble for him. Adam adjusts his tie as he jogs upstairs to meet Eve. Adam sees Eve dressed in revealing sexy lingerie, that he has never seen before and is breath taken. She puts her finger to his mouth to keep him quiet as she blind folds him and wraps his wrist with a sash. Eve takes off Adam's clothes piece by piece while slowly caressing his body. She quietly signals for Indigo to take her place in seducing her husband as she watches. Adam is curious because he recognizes that this touch doesn't feel like Eve's.

"Eve, what's going on? Take this blindfold off of me....now", he states hesitantly while enjoying the familiar taste of Indigo's kiss.

"Are you sure?" Eve asks while being internally tickled.

"Yeah, Adam are you sure?" Indigo laughs.

Indigo's voice sounds very recognizable to Adam. Nevertheless, he thinks it unbelievable to imagine Taipan is seducing him, and Eve is allowing it.

"Taipan? Eve, take this blindfold off of me and untie me," Adam states confused.

"Ok, if you insist," Eve says and follows Adam's command.

Eve unties Adam and takes off his blindfold. Adam looks at Eve and then in awe at Taipan AKA Indigo's direction.

"What in the hell is all of this and how do you know Taipan. Baby, what has gotten into you?" Adam questions with bewilderment and waits for further understanding.

Eve takes Adam's hand and escorts him into the bathroom for some privacy.

"Remember you told me that you would do anything for me to make up for neglecting me? Well, this is how you can make it up to me," Eve explains holding both of Adam's hands.

Adam shakes his head with a look of confusion and wonders if this is really his wife in front of him.

"Really! How do you know my coworker Taipan?" Adam asks while scratching his head.

"Who is Taipan?" Eve asks for clarification as she looks through Adam.

"The lady you have in our bedroom with us works with me at Uniquely Designed on the global account," Adam plainly explains while pointing in the direction of their bedroom.

Eve sits down on the edge of the tub, puts her hand on her forehead and snickers.

Eve shakes her head and smirks, "She told me her name was Indigo, because I am not supposed to know her real name. I can explain all of this to you in the morning. Let's just enjoy this night and just give into what you are feeling. I know you are attracted to her because your body doesn't lie."

Adam thinks for a minute before speaking as a picture of Taipan bending down and licking her lips while in the office came to mind.

"Ok, if you insist, I will do it for you," Adam fronts as though he obliging to fulfill Eve's passionate desires.

Adam and Eve reenter the bedroom with Taipan. Adam looks Taipan in the eyes and they all pick up where they left off. Early the next morning, Taipan had already let herself out of the house. Adam and Eve woke up, turned towards each other with smiles as they began to discuss last night events.

"Good morning, Tiger," Adam states with a whipped look on his face.

"Good morning! So, I guess the expression on your face you means that you enjoyed yourself last night," Eve acknowledges while shaking her head up and down as she grins.

"Yeah, it was pretty cool," Adam retorts as he reminisces.

"Adam, I feel so free, since I have been doing this," Eve explains in exhilaration.

"Eve, how long have you been doing this and how do you know Taipan?" Adam asks inquisitively while moving Eve's hair to showcase her eyes.

"I have known Indigo AKA Taipan for about three months now," she reveals rubbing Adam's arm.

The doorbell rings. Adam and Eve look at each other and walk over to the intercom.

"Adam and Eve, where are you?" The Father demands an answer.

They ignore his call and look at each other perplexed. Then the father calls again.

"Adam and Eve, where are you? Now, you know that I know you are in there. What is taking you so long to answer?" He roars as He questions.

Adam and Eve look at each other with guilt and shame.

"We are naked. Let us put some clothes on and we will be right down to answer the door," Adam replies while they rush to cover up their nakedness.

"Mmmmhmm, I see. So you're naked," the Father responds knowingly.

"When was the last time you spoke with Dad," Adam inquires with apprehension covering up his nakedness.

Eve shrugs her shoulders with a guilty look on her face as she covers her exposed body.

"It's been long time since I've spoken with either of you. Now, please open your door," The Father states gently.

With the intercom still on, they look at each other shaking their heads. Adam and Eve go downstairs to open the door for their father.

"How are you doing? Is this a bad time for you? I just came by to check on you and to see how you were doing," the Father states with obvious disappointment.

Adam and Eve are distant to the father. They want him to leave because they feel quite awkward in his presence.

"Don't answer all at once," He raises his voice as he looks at both of them, as they avoid contact with the father.

"I have been working long hours at the office for the You Name It Project on which I have been diligently working. What about you Eve? What have you been up to lately?" Adam directs the question to Eve as he taps her and stares at the ground.

"Mmmmhmmm! Oh, I seeee, son! You have been just exerting all your time in the You Name It Project. Ok, I see, son. And, my daughter, my firstborn daughter Eve what have you been doing lately?" he discontentedly asks while shaking his head.

Eve answered reluctantly having been placed on the spot, "I have been doing a little bit of this and a little bit of that."

"Oh, I see....little bit of this and that! Well, I just wanted to check up on you. Please call me when you have the time to fit me into your busy schedule. Now remember, no matter what happens nothing can ever separate you from my love. I am going to leave you to carry on with your activities," He states and leaves their house.

Once the father leaves, Adam and Eve putting their heads in their hands soak in their guilt and shame.

CHAPTER 10

BEAT IT

> "Behold, I have given you authority to trample on serpents and scorpions, and over all the power of the enemy" -Luke 10:19 NKJV

Over the next few days, as Adam and Eve perform their weekly duties they reminisce over their actions. They also consider unanswered questions pertaining to their newfound sexual interest. These thoughts cause divisiveness in their friendships as well as in their marriage. Eve begins to think more and more about Taipan's actions and ignores her calls. Adam also avoids Taipan at work as best he can. As Adam thinks more about Eve's actions, their sex life dwindles to nothing even when Eve initiates intimacy.

While they are eating dinner Eve begins to ask Adam questions about Taipan.

"Eve, we need to talk," he says gently while rubbing his head.

"Yes, we do," Eve states softly with tears in her eyes.

"You can start with any questions you have. Let's be honest even if it's difficult and it hurts," Adam says with sincerity.

"So, I keep thinking about Taipan. How close did the two of you work together?" she asks calmly with a serious look on her face.

"We work closely with each other because she assists me with the You Name It Project," he shares honestly as he stares at Eve.

Did she know that you were married and that you were married to me?" she inquires with a stern look on her face becoming angry.

"Yes, she did. I have a picture of me and you on my desk and she complimented your beauty. She knew that I was married to you," Adam admits while holding Eve's hands to bring down her rising temperature.

"Oh, I see! So you were attracted to her before I brought her in our home. Is there anything I should know?" Eve's voice escalating while aggressively pulling her hands away from Adam's.

Eve stands up and paces the floor.

"There is one more thing. She kissed me at work after we were promoted," he shares in a low tone with his head bowed down.

"Adam don't make it seem like you just stood there and didn't kiss her back. I could tell you were so attracted to her when she first touched you. Please get out of my face. This discussion is over. How could you?!" Eve yells and storms upstairs to their bedroom.

Adam follows her up the stairs and opens the door Eve had just slammed.

"Oh, Eve this conversation is just getting started. Were there more lovers than just Taipan?" Adam asks with his hand holding open their bedroom door.

Eve paused a long time before answering.

"Yes," she states remorsefully.

"Men, too?!" Adam asks angrily raising his voice and face turning red.

Eve nods and cries. Adam walks away, goes downstairs as Eve follows..

"I am not the only one at fault," Eve cries hysterically.

During the night Adam and Eve are in bed sleeping with their backs towards each other. Adam leaves the bedroom and sleeps on the couch downstairs.

Boa's Studio Apartment

Eve makes an unexpected visit to Boa's home without calling him first. Taipan is at his house when Boa answers the door.

"Hey, come on in," he smirks. "Indigo is here, too. Why don't you make yourself comfortable," he offers in anticipation of having a sexual encounter.

"Definitely not! It's not that type of party," she snaps, mugs and take off her earrings.

"Hey, girl! Where have you been? I have been calling and leaving messages trying to contact you. Where have you been…with your man? Girl, that was such a coincidence that we work together. You are a blessed woman," she mentions smiling and shaking her head.

Eve grabs Taipan by her head and throws her on the ground. Taipan lands on her stomach and begins to attempt to crawl away. Eve catches her and begins to stomp Taipan with her foot. Boa stops Eve from injuring Taipan's head.

"Eve, I am sorry this has happened to you. I didn't know she would stoop that low to do such a thing. I promise you I didn't have anything to do with this," he says sincerely.

"You were probably being deceptive as well!" Eve yells in Boa's face.

"Ok, the truth is I am a D.C. native, born and raised. I graduated from Ballou High School. My goal was to tap that," he swears as he raises his right hand.

Eve shrieks, quickly turns, and walks out of the door.

Adam's Job Uniquely Designed

Adam is called into the boss's office.

"Have a seat, Adam," Mr. King directs while holding his hand toward an empty chair.

"How are you doing, Sir?" Adam asks as he sits down.

Mr. King begins, "Let's cut to the chase! Aaaahhh, I have some disappointing news that I must share with you. There are pictures of you, Taipan and your wife circulating around our client's offices as well as the companies in which we are marketing the You Name It Project. You did an outstanding job! But, I am going to have to let Taipan go, and only because you have been with me from the start of this business will I allow you to stay. Nevertheless, you will be demoted. That means your salary will be cut as well," he states regretfully looking into Adam's eyes.

Adam silently sinks back into his seat putting his hand on his head.

"How did this happen?" Adam questions slowly..

Mr. King comes from behind his desk, sits on the edge of his desk and leans in closer to Adam.

Mr. King says to Adam, "You know I consider you my son. What were you thinking? You are a married man to one wife. What were you and Eve both thinking? How did you get pulled into such a situation? Think long but don't think wrong. You have a beautiful wife who loves you dearly. That didn't even look like sweet Eve in the video. Now, you know I seen it. Something was different in Eve's eyes. What was really going on?" Mr. King asks but in a scolding tone.

"Eve wanted to reward me for my promotion and thought I would like company in our bedroom with another beautiful woman. So, she brought Taipan to our home not knowing that she was my coworker. I truly apologize for letting you down," Adam explains sorrowfully covering his face and shaking his head.

"You're sorry for letting me down. Son, see it's deeper than you just letting me down. You let your wife down and even more than that you let your Father down. You have to keep your priorities straight. That means God, your wife and then work. How is Eve doing with all of this?" Mr. King asks truly concerned..

"You remind me sooo much of my Father when you speak. Eve is hurting because of my response to the things she has done to me. I neglected her and put her second to my work, therefore she sought love from all the wrong places. How foolish could I be to do that to my precious Eve? I wasn't covering her the way I should.

I am going to make it right," Adam admits truthfully wiping tears from his face.

Mr. King continued, "I hired someone to investigate Ms.Taipan. She was the one who recorded your sexual rendezvous and sent it to our clients. I don't know why because it caused her to lose her job with us. The PI told me when he saw her the other day her face was all bruised up and her head had gauze wrapped all around it. Who knows? This definitely was not her first rodeo. She is single and preys on married men. She has been successful in her career but was treated harshly by some lover in the past and that scarred her. She is a walking threat to married women because she wants what they have. By the way, I saw you staring at her peach on numerous occasions. Nevertheless, and I mean nevertheless, We all sin and fall short of the glory of God. Listen, take a few days off from work to get yourself together as well as to straighten out everything at home. Pray with Eve, and I will be praying for you! Then, when you come back we can talk about your new assignment," Mr. King concluded and gave Adam dap and a hug.

"Thank you for being a true friend, Mr. King," Adam stated with a regretful side smirk as he stood up from his chair.

Adam walked out of Mr. King office.

Chapter 11

Loving You

"Let marriage be held in honor among all,"
-Hebrews 13:4 ESV

Adam and Eve's House

Adam walks in the door, and Eve is sitting on the couch soaking her feet. Adam begins to shake his head.

"Do you mind if I massage your feet for you? Awww, sweetheart your heel is bruised," he kneels and kisses her feet. Evie Eve, what have you been up to?" he asks looking at her from the corner of his eye.

"I have been just trying to make things right. I have been acting like I lost my everlasting mind. When I was presented with the opportunity I should have never given in to the temptation no matter how fulfilling it looked to me at the time," Eve states disappointedly looking at the floor.

"Eve, don't beat yourself up like that. If I didn't neglect you and your needs, I doubt if you would have given into that snake's advances. I must be honest though; I am having a problem in my mind handling the fact that you were intimate with other men. I don't know if it is my ego or what, Babe," he expresses truthfully with tears in his eyes.

"Baby, no one can love me better than you can. If I could go back in time I would not have messed with that man….them men…..and women," she professes thinking with her fist on her chin.

Eve wraps her arms around Adam and kisses the top of his head. She sings *No One Compares to the Man I Got*. Just then, the doorbell rings and Adam presses the intercom. It is the father at the door.

"It's so good to see you!" he cries while giving The Father dap and a hug.

"It's good to see you too my son, and you opened your door when I rang the doorbell the first time," he acknowledges hugging him tightly.

Eve runs to greet the father.

"Hey, Daddy! Oh, how I have missed you," she cries holding him intimately.

"Now, that's what I expect from my daughter!" He smiles ever so brightly while embracing Eve.

Adam and Eve pray together. Adam now works three different jobs, nevertheless he makes time to spend time with his wife and meets her needs. They attend marital counseling to work on their issues that resulted from sinning. Eve visits the gynecologist and is informed that she is pregnant. Nine months later, in excruciating pain, she gives birth to a baby boy.

Grocery Store

"Remember, our choices as wives and mothers have repercussions that can affect us, our husbands, children, and those attached to us for either good or bad. The enemy comes to steal, kill, and destroy. That's his job and the enemy is cunning. It is our job not to act out of our feelings for temporary satisfaction. Our actions can either bring life or death to us as well as to others. God creates us as helpmates that reproduce good fruit, Chile," Eve states while getting happy and praising God!

"Yesssss! I totally hear you," Bathsheba agrees and nods her head.

Bathsheba waves to get the waiter's attention. The handsome waiter comes to the table and licks his lips while looking at Bathsheba intently in her eyes.

"How may I help you?" the waiter questions flirting with Bathsheba.

"Please, take the apple pie off of my order. I definitely don't want that," Bathsheba states seriously, mugs and shakes her head.

Bathsheba shakes her head with a stank face and Eve laughs!

Eve and Bathsheba are eating bread and drinking red wine.

"Dang, I am sorry you experienced all of that. What happened next? Did life get better for the both of you?" Bathsheba curiously asks with both hands on the sides of her face.

"Hmmmm! Did life get better? Well, for starters, we had to move out of our beautiful place in Eden. Then, years later, my son whom I loved dearly was killed intentionally by his own brother. Remember it's all about the choices you make," Eve states slowly while shaking her head.

Eve takes a sip of her red wine.

Correctional Facility

"So, that is the story of Eve. Now, she was the first of many," Deborah concluded while clapping her hands.

"Mrs. Deborah, I have to put some respect on that name! That was an amazing story," Cassandra compliments shaking her head in awe.

"You can read plenty of exciting stories like this in the Bible that relate to what you experience in today's times. Y'all, there ain't nothing under the sun that hasn't been done before. What you see and endure today just has a more modern twist to it," Deborah explains sassily as she points her finger and shakes her head.

The inmates praise Deborah's keep it real story telling and ask her to tell another story. Deborah pulls her hair up into a bun and rolls her sleeves up before she starts the next story.

"Ok, ok ,ok ….since you asked for it! Now, this next story will knock you off your feet. There was a young lady named Bathsheba who was a married woman; whose one major decision would change the whole trajectory of her life," Deborah narrates with a suspenseful tone and accenting hand gestures.

Chapter 12

Fight The Power

"For the weapons of our warfare are not of the flesh but have divine power to destroy strongholds"
-2 Corinthians 10:4

The Protest

(Instrumental version of Fight the Power is playing)

Uriah, a young, brave soldier with a caramel complexion, was placed on the frontline of the protest carrying a bull horn. As he marched, the soldiers with him held up signs that had the names of individuals who were slain senselessly. The names were: Emmett Till, Breonna Taylor, George Floyd, Trayvon Martin, Michael Brown, Eric Gray and many others.

"We won't be oppressed any longer! We won't be enslaved in our minds! We will be everything that we are called to be! The victory is ours! We will prosper and move forward to take what rightfully belongs to us! You can try to stop us but we will succeed by any means necessary!"

The soldiers who were with Uriah were amped up and began to shout loudly and pump their fists and signs in the air. As the army was moving forward, a bullet hit Uriah in his heart and he fell face forward onto the ground. The soldiers trampled over Uriah's body as they moved forward to conquer the territory. Uriah passionately screamed his last words through his bull horn!

Eden's

Television screen at Eden's, a soul food restaurant with vegan alternatives, located in the heart of D.C., highlights a breaking news story that Uriah was killed in the front line of a battle.

"My word! When is it going to stop! I have to check on Bathsheba. I hope she is ok. These killings are so senseless and it makes me sick!" she said as she dials the phone.

Bathsheba's House

Bathsheba is taking a bath while looking at television. A breaking news report confirms one of the bodies in last night's tragic shooting at the protest held in Washington, D.C. has been identified. The person identified was Uriah, an elite soldier, in his early twenties. The sound of the reporter's voice fades as Bathsheba digests the news of her husband's death.

"Uri, no, no no no, Uri. What have I done?!" Bathsheba cries rubbing her belly.

A picture of Bathsheba and Uriah smiling is on a nearby table.

Eden's

Eve dials Bathsheba, her call is picked up by the answering machine and she listens to the recorded message.

"You have reached Uri and Sheba! We aren't available to answer your call at this time but will return your call as soon as we can. Please leave a message after the beep and have a wonderful day!" they say in unison with laughter in their voices.

Eve and Sheba both hear the message at their locations.

"Sheba, this is Eve. I am worried about you. Call me back or I am on my way over to your house. Bathsheba isn't answering the phone. I hope she is ok. I have to go check on her, Gabriella. Please hold down the fort while I am gone," she says worriedly while taking off her apron.

"Ok! Sheba is going to be alright. Here, take her something to eat and drive safely," Gabriella says with compassion looking into Eve's eyes.

"Thank you! I surely hope so," she says shaking her head.

Gabriella hands Eve a packed bag of food and Eve walks out of the restaurant briskly.

Bathsheba's House

"Why? Why did this have to happen to me?" she cries hysterically and hears the doorbell rings.

"Go away!" Bathsheba screams.

"It's Eve. Now, you know I am not going anywhere until you open the door. I am worried about you! Open the door, Sheba!" she says with a raised voice.

Bathsheba opens the door in her sweat clothes with her hair all over her head. Eve notices that the house is dark with no lights on and with the shades drawn.

"I am here," Eve says wrapping her arms around Bathsheba who continues to cry uncontrollably.

"I know you haven't been eating so I brought you one of your favorite meals. Yes, it's curry chicken," she says putting the food down on the table.

Bathsheba did not respond but walked over to the couch. She plopped down and pulled the covers over her body. Eve sat down beside her and Bathsheba used Eve's lap as a pillow. Eve rubs Bathsheba's head gently while Bathsheba wipes the tears from her face. The next morning, Eve cleans up Bathsheba's house and opens the blinds to allow the natural sun light to enter the house. Bathsheba opens her puffy eyes, yawns, and stretches with her arms reaching toward the sky.

"Good morning, Sunshine. Weeping endures for a night but joy comes in the morning," she smiles a Eve holding out a plate of food.

Eve hands the food and a fork to Bathsheba who receives the plate with a frowned faced. "Eve what is this you are serving me it smells awful," she states with a look of disgust.

"Now, I know you absolutely love my curry chicken so just take a bite of it," Eve nudges giving Bathsheba the side eye.

Bathsheba takes a bite of the curry chicken and vomits it out into the trash can that's filled with the tissue she used to wipe her tears.

"Something is not right with this chicken! This does not taste anything like the curry that you make for me," she says wiping her mouth.

"Is it really something wrong with my curry or is it something wrong with you? I had a plate of the curry while you were sleeping. I am not tooting my own horn or anything but it's really good, Sheba," Eve stated with her hand on her hip.

Bathsheba turned her head in the opposite direction of Eve with a look of gloom.

"I know what the issue is. I am pregnant," she stated remorsefully with her lifeless eyes looking toward the ground.

"Congratulations! Now, that makes perfectly good sense. I was the same way when I was pregnant with my children. Whew, the births of my children were something else, but it's temporary. At least you will have a child to remind you of Uriah. How sweet," Eve thought as she spoke.

There was not a mumbling word from Bathsheba for about 30 seconds. The room is completely silent. Finally, Bathsheba slowly speaks but looking away from Eve, " The baby isn't Uriah's….."

Bathsheba looked at Eve from the corner of her eye. Eve took a load off her feet as she processed the information that Bathsheba revealed.

"Do you know who the baby's father is?" Eve inquires in a low tone.

"Mmmmhmm," she mumbled while looking in the opposite direction of Eve.

"I see. You know you are in a no judgment zone with me. Who's is it?" she asked curiously.

Bathsheba was silent a few seconds before responding.

"It's David, Jesse's son," she said with an ashamed countenance.

Eve put her hand on her on forehead, bowed her head and began to shake her head.

"My word. David. Mmmmm hmm. I see. David. I hear that he is not the one to be played with. Please tell me how you have gotten into this situation here. Don't spare any details and don't leave out anything," she insists.

"I take the blame because although you talked to me in the store and told me your story I still acted out of my loneliness," she confesses tears dripping from her eyes.

Chapter 13

Self-Destruction

"Do not let you adornment be merely outward"
-1 Peter 3:3 ESV

Mirage Night Club

Tia, a beautiful snicker doodle complexioned woman in her early twenties, with sandy brown natural hair and a killer body, invited Bathsheba to the club to get some much needed attention.

"Girl, I am so glad you decided to come to work with me instead of staying up in the house all lonely and stuff. Girl, you should get out and have some fun while making your own coin. You heard me?" Tia stated boldly.

"Yeah, I heard ya', but I am kind of nervous. I have never done anything like this before," Eve says with her voice shaking.

"You are going to be alright, because they know me up in this joint. The celebrities and all of them are going to want you. Girl, you are beautiful and have that bomb shape too. Boo, you are going to be good. You trust me right?" she asks smacking her on the butt.

"Yeah, I trust you. What can it hurt?" she says with a little more confidence but still with a quiver in her voice.

They walk into the club and Tia introduces Bathsheba to Los, the arrogant and boisterous club owner with an obvious Napoleon syndrome.

"It's nice to meet you, Beautiful! Turn around so I can see all of you," Los states licking his lips.

Bathsheba turns around hesitantly.

"Yes, sir! Mmmmmhmmm! You my dear will be a great addition to this club. We have some celebrity guests coming in here tonight. I want you on the top floor with Tia and use whatever props you like. Give these dudes the show and time of their lives. This club ain't called the Mirage for nothing. Get to work!" he says authoritatively.

Bathsheba and Tia go to the dressing room and put on their fanciest stripper attire. Bathsheba picks out her props and tells the engineer what she requires to make her vision come to life. At this time the Mirage is fully packed. Tia dances and comes back to the dressing room with racks of cash. Next up it's Bathsheba's turn to perform, the lights are dim and she is sitting on a chair. The spotlight shines.on her and she begins to exotically dance on and around the chair. The audience cheers as Bathsheba takes off her matching blinged out bra top and thong piece by piece while dancing seductively. The crowd roars and throws cash on the stage left and right. Bathsheba prepares for the finale as she sits her nude body in the chair and picks up a loofah. A bucket of soapy water falls from above saturating her whole body. She washes from the top of her hair to the bottom of her feet. The crowd roars, jumps up and down and throw money from every direction onto the stage. Bathsheba catches the eye and attention of a fine man named David.

"Hey, who is that?" he inquisitively asked the men, who were with him.

Mike, David's fine chocolate skinned chauffeur and one of the men with David responded factually, "Bathsheba is Uriah' s wife and Elian's daughter from around the way. Man, you don't remember? Bathsheba... Lil' Sheba? Yeah, she's all grown up now, though.

Bathsheba and Tia leave the club.

"Girrrrl, you are a natural! You did your thing out there, tonight. How was it...bathing in the nude and all.

Yous a wild girl," Tia states cracking up and popping her gum.

"It wasn't bad at all. I got so much attention, Girl," she reminisces.

"What did you expect by bathing in the nude publicly? Inquiring minds want to know," she laughs.

"I guess you have a point there," she said while smiling and laughing.

Bathsheba and Tia continue to laugh and talk while walking in the direction of their car. A limousine drives up and the chauffeur opens his door and walks over to Bathsheba.

"Hello, David would like to make your acquaintance and he requests an opportunity to get to know you better," he states as he bows.

"Who is David?" they ask simultaneously.

"Bathsheba, you know David. He is a real good dude and rumor has it that he is a man after God's own heart," he adamantly states licking his lips and patting his heart.

Bathsheba smiles and blushes.

"Dang, Sheba! It seems like the real attention you want is just getting started. Are you going to go with him? You don't even know him at all," she states worriedly but excitedly.

"I assure you of Bathsheba's safety. She will have a good time and be well cared for," Mike reassures.

"You look like you want to go, but once again you do not know them like that. Do you have mace? I am so for real right now. Please be safe and call me if you need anything and send me your location," Tia instructs.

"Ok, I will," Bathsheba says as she walks towards the limousine.

When Bathsheba enters the limousine, David is inside awaiting her arrival. She sits across from David he admires her beauty while drinking wine and eating caviar.

"You're even better looking up close. I am David, and it's a pleasure to meet you. Help yourself to some wine and caviar," he says sensually.

"No, thank you! So, you're David, a man after God's own heart!" she chuckles and smiles looking into his eyes.

"Where to boss?" Mike asks.

"The palace," David says staring into Bathsheba's eyes.

Bathsheba scrolls through her cellphone and looks out the window to keep David from noticing that she is blushing. David continues to stare, captivated by Bathsheba's beauty.

David's Palace

David and Bathsheba arrive at the palace. Bathsheba's eyes light up when she sees the beautifully constructed home. David smirks and shakes his head. Bathsheba struts and follows Mike as she walks into the palace. David walks behind her adoring her assets. They make themselves comfortable in David's family room, and David's servants shut the door behind them for privacy.

"Can I get you anything else before I retire for the evening sir?" Mike humbly asks

"That will be all for the evening. Thank you, Mike, and be safe," David says as they hug and dap each other up.

Mike leaves and closes the doors behind him.

"Your home is simply amazing! I love your choice of art as well as your décor selections. You must have had an interior decorator," she states as she walks around in admiration.

"I actually claim ownership for the ideas for the palace but had the best skilled experts bring my vision to life. Would you like a glass of wine?" He made his claim confidently while drinking his wine.

"So, you are a visionary, handsome, powerful, and considered to be the man! What else should I know about you David? What are your interests and what do you like to do for fun other than bringing women you barely know to your home?" she asks in a sexy tone while wiping the sleep from David's eye.

Bathsheba was attracted to David's handsome look, swag and confident eyes which carried a hint of sadness. She walked away from David's personal space and poured herself a glass of wine. David's eyes followed Bathsheba's every step and every graceful move she made. He was smitten and extremely attracted to her.

"Well, I love to write music, play instruments and sing. These are some of the things I enjoy. What makes you think I am powerful?" he asks smiling and gazing into her eyes.

"This wine is really good! Your reputation precedes itself. I have heard about how you conquered that giant who threatened to enslave our people, and I have heard the songs that the women sing about you. Saul has killed his thousands and David his ten thousands. I have also heard that you are a man who gets what he wants by any means necessary," she states as she turns in his direction while sipping on her glass of wine.

David blushes, smiles, pours another glass of wine and states, "I see you keep your ears to the streets. I must admit you are a visionary yourself the way you performed tonight."

David walked up close to Bathsheba and noticed the confident look in her eyes which also contained hint of sadness. They see in each other's eyes the familiar void they each wish was filled. In silence, they stare at each other without interruption for a few moments. David strokes the side of Bathsheba's face gently and the hairs on Bathsheba's arms rise.. She walks away quickly and takes a huge gulp of her wine.

So, what made you decide to take except my offer to come to my place?" David inquires.

Bathsheba turns in David's direction and stares into his eyes intently. She walks slowly in David's direction to where he is sitting in a chair.

"I told you earlier that you are powerful…..didn't I? You have the power and the authority to get anything you want. So, I decided to make it easy for you," she states and takes off all of her clothes, except for her red matching undergarments and straddles David with one leg.

David and Bathsheba kiss, caress and make love until the early morning. Bathsheba showers and Mike escorts her home. Bathsheba plays the events over and over in her mind.

Chapter 14

No, No, No, No, No

"You shall not commit adultery"
-Exodus 20:14 NKJV

Bathsheba's House

Bathsheba is upstairs in her bedroom and the phone rings. Bathsheba runs to grab and answer her phone.

"Hey, Tia! What's up! How are you doing?" Bathsheba asks.

"Hey, girl! No, the question is what's up with you? How did everything go last night. Girl, David is a boss! Tell me how did it go? " Tia asks smiling.

"All I have to say is that he is a really nice guy and a straight gentleman," she says quickly.

"Ok, I hear you Sheba. So, what's up with Mike? Is he single? Oh, I guess that really doesn't matter when you messin' with ballers these days," she states and cracks up laughing.

"Tia, you're not funny at all. I have to go, because I think Uri just walked through the door," she whispers and rushes to get off the phone.

"Ok, I will talk to you later and don't forget to see what's up with Mike for a sistah," she says quickly.

"Ok, bye, T," she replies quickly and hangs up the phone.

Bathsheba looks in the mirror and straightens herself up.

"Uri, is that you?" she yells downstairs.

"Yeah, Sheba. I'm home," he states sadly.

Bathsheba runs downstairs and gives Uriah a huge welcoming hug. Uriah barely hugs her back. Bathsheba rolls her eyes while hugging Uriah tightly.

"Have a seat Babe and take a load off of your feet. I am going to cook your favorite meal, and we can spend some much needed time together. Let me cater to my man," she states enthusiastically.

"No, I am going to take a shower, and then see what else I can do to help out my brothers who are still at war," he states tiredly but with dedication.

Uriah walks upstairs to take his shower and Bathsheba plops down in the couch.

Bathsheba's House- A Month Later

Bathsheba looks in the calendar on her Apple iPhone and notices that she has not received her menstrual cycle this month. She begins to recall the night that she shared with David and sits down on her bed. Bathsheba orders a pregnancy test from Insta Cart, and when it arrives she administers the test. Bathsheba's first and second results are positive. She plops down on her bed in utter shock.

"What am I going to do? Uriah….," she says to herself shaking her head.

Bathsheba calls David. The phone rings and David picks up.

"Hello," he answers.

"Hey! I need to see you immediately!" she declares anxiously and paces the floor as she speaks.

"Bet! I've missed you and have been wanting to see you too," he says smiling.

"No, it's not like that. I mean it's an emergency!" she cries without restraint.

"Sheba, are you ok? I will send a driver to you immediately," he says now concerned.

"No, I am not ok, but I will drive. I am on my way," she insists.

"Ok, I am waiting for you," he says and hangs up the phone.

Bathsheba puts on her shoes. She puts the tests in a plastic bag and places them in her purse. Bathsheba hurriedly drives over to David's house.

David's Palace

He is at the front entrance expecting her arrival. She walks in the house and they go to a private location in the palace. They hug each other tightly and as they separate David is still holding Bathsheba's extended arms in a gentle fashion.

"What's wrong?" he asks in a caring tone.

Bathsheba cries as she reaches into her purse, pulls out the pregnancy tests and hands them to David. David reads the results as he sits down in his chair.

"I don't mean to be disrespectful, but I have to ask the question. Are you sure that it's mine?" he asks gently.

"I actually understand your questioning. Who wouldn't want to get knocked up by David The Powerful Man of God. That's not my MO. I haven't been with Uriah for months nor any other man for that matter," she states angrily and then sits down beside him.

"So now that the baby is mine can we do it again?" he asks with an inviting grin.

"No, are you crazy? This is serious! What about my husband?" she yells and cries.

"Yeah, I am little crazy sometimes, but I understand where you are coming from. Don't worry! I will work everything out. I promise. Don't you worry your pretty little face off," he states while hugging her and stroking her hair.

Bathsheba leaves David's palace and returns home. David begins to conjure up a plan.

Chapter 15

You So Evil

"They hold fast to the evil purpose, they talk of laying snares secretly, thinking, "Who can see them?" -Psalm 64:5 ESV

David's Palace

David picks up the phone and makes a phone call to Joab, the dark chocolate skinned, muscular commander of David's army."Hey, man," He greets in a somber tone while biting his nails as he cozies up next to his fireplace.

"What's up, Dave?" Joab curiously replies while reviewing the strategic paperwork for the march.

"Jo, I need you to come by my crib as soon as possible," he commands in an urgent tone.

"I am own my way," he replies and rushes to get into his vehicle.

They hang up the phone and Joab proceeds to David's palace immediately. Joab arrives at David's palace in less than 30 minutes.

"I rushed over here as fast I could after our phone call. Why the urgency? Is anything wrong?" he asks worriedly.

"I tell you Jo if it ain't one thing it's another. It's not to much too handle, but I just need your help with a slight issue," he says calmly.

"Just say the word and I will handle it. What do you need?" he reassures with a nod of his head.

"Tell me everything you know about Uriah," he insists.

"Uriah is real good people. He is loyal and passionate about our cause. He is a true, dependable soldier that gets the job done. He is married to Bathsheba, Eliam's daughter," he states convincingly.

"I would love to meet him. Please bring him to me," David directs.

"Sure thing! I will call him now. He doesn't live far from here," Joab states as he picks up the phone to call Uriah.

Uriah's phone rings.

"Hey, what's up, Jo?" Uriah answers with a grin.

"Hey, man! Where are you? I need you to come to David's place. He wants to meet you. How long will it take for you to get here?" Joab presses.

"I am right around the corner at a Black Lives Matter meeting. I can be there in about 20 minutes," he expresses passionately.

"Ok, bet! I will see you in a few minutes," he says.

"Bet," he responds.

"Joab echoes, "He will be here in a few minutes. He is a real good dude. You will see what I am talking about when you meet him." he states while nodding his head.

"I take your word for it," David says as he strokes his beard.

Uriah arrives at David's palace, and Joab walks Uriah into David's office.

Joab introduces the brothers, "David this is Uriah and Uriah this is David."

David and Uriah shake hands.

"It's nice to meet you brother. I commend you for hard work fighting for justice in our community", David compliments.

"Likewise, brother! It sickens me to my stomach that families are losing loved ones for no apparent reason. Children are forced to grow up without parents and parents are grieving over the tragic and unnecessary death of their children. If I don't fight for our rights who will?!" he states passionately.

"Jo, he is the real deal! Uriah, I appreciate how much time you are spending for the betterment of our community, but everybody needs a break now and then. Take the rest of the day off. Spend some time with your wife," David encourages.

"Thanks, David. You are the real one. It was really nice meeting you. Stay tight," he states as they hug and dap..

"Man, let me walk you out," he states walking towards the office door.

Uriah leaves the palace and David calls one of his servants over the intercom.

"Hey, please place an order from Ruth Chris Steakhouse and have it delivered to Uriah's home by 8:00 P.M. Please order the best lobster and steak meal offered. Pair it with my favorite bottle of Cabernet Sauvignon. Joab has Uriah's address."

"Will do," the female assistant affirms in her accented voice.

"Thank you," he says gratefully.

Later in the evening, David is in his robe and lying in his bed when the butler calls on the intercom.

"David, the man who was with Joab earlier in your office is sleeping on the front stairs of the palace," the butler states over the intercom in a confused manner.

David looks around and is puzzled.

"This dude," David states while getting out of bed to put on his slippers.

David goes to the front of the palace where Uriah is sleeping.

"Man, what are you doing out here? I thought you were supposed to be home having a good meal, relaxing, unwinding and enjoying your wife," he inquires.

Bathsheba's House

Bathsheba is sitting at the table filled with food from Ruth Chris Steakhouse that David had ordered. She is dressed in sexy lingerie, sipping on a glass of wine, and waiting for Uriah to come home looking disappointed.

David's Palace

"I had no other place to go. After I left your home earlier, I went back to my meeting. After we addressed community issues and devised strategic plans to combat the opposition's efforts, I began thinking in-depth about how every time I turn on the news I hear about another tragedy that has impacted our community. I just feel like

I am not doing enough, and it plays on my mind and my heart," he explains wiping a tear from his eyes.

"I understand. Man, you need to get some rest and take a load off of your mind. Come inside and sleep in one of the guest rooms tonight. Get a fresh start in the morning. You might even need to see a therapist," he offers acting concerned about Uriah's grief.

"Thank you! You are a real one," he replies and grins as he stands up.

David holds the door for Uriah to come into the house and has a servant to show Uriah to the room where he will sleep. The next evening, Uriah is still at David's house. When David sees Uriah at the palace, he begins to scratch his head in contemplation.

"So how are you feeling today?" he asks with suspicion.

"I have so much on my mind that it's difficult for me to rest," he cries while rubbing his head.

"Let's talk about this more over dinner. You deserve a good meal and my chef makes the best lamb chops in the world with a tasty dipping sauce," he describes while putting his arm around Uriah's shoulders.

David escorts Uriah into the dining room.

"Please give Uriah the best wine we have in the house. *Mi casa es su casa*. Man, you have to try the lamb chops," he states with a grin and raised hands.

"Bruh, thank you for your kindness. I can't eat and I can't sleep at night. I have dreams about our brothers and sisters being slain senselessly. What kind of man would I be if I am at home eating good meals and enjoying my wife while my brothers are preparing to go to battle. Naw, that doesn't even make sense to me. That's why I don't go home," he vents passionately with a tear in his eye.

"Pour my man another glass. Please continue where you left off. The reason why you don't go home….," he instructs while chewing his food and waving his utensils with his napkin tucked into his shirt.

"Innocent people are dying brutally, and Bruh, you know what hurts my heart the most? I hate to see our brothers killing each other. We have to diffuse the powers of Willie Lynch and Jim Crow. If I don't fight for justice or to better our community, their blood is on my hands. I need to fight with them. Brother, it is my duty to serve," he boldly and emotionally declares as he gulped his wine.

"I love your passion and that's why we are honoring you this evening. Pour my man another glass and keep the wine coming. We appreciate you, your dedication and loyalty. To Uriah!" he cheers as he holds up his glass.

David and Uriah toast their glasses together, continue to drink and converse over dinner. After dinner, David tells his driver to take Uriah home in an attempt to make him spend intimate time with his wife. David retires to bed and wakes up early the next morning to see that Uriah never left the palace.

"This dude here," he states grinding his teeth on the verge of having a tantrum.

David calls Joab over to the palace, and Joab arrives shortly after.

"Hey, Dave! What do you need, boss? Oh, before I forget, I told you Uriah was good peoples. He's a soldier for real. So, tell me, what did you think about him?" he asks excitedly with a huge grin.

"Yeah, I agree that he is a true soldier that I want on the front lines. I believe with his skill level and passion that that is where we need to position him," he states adamantly.

Joab's huge grin quickly turns to a frown with an intense mug after hearing David's positioning assignment for Uriah.

"You know that's where the battle is the fiercest, and he could possibly get seriously injured or killed," Joab raises his tone.

"Man, stand down and stop mugging me! I know you admire the brother's servitude, and I know this assignment is risky. But, if anything should happen to him, I will make sure that I personally take care of his wife. I promise," David plots while checking Brother Jo.

"Are you sure you thought this strategy through? Uriah is a good dude Dave," he humbly asks.

"I did, so, Jo, just please do what I have asked of you," he calmly states while looking at the paperwork on his desk.

"Will do," he obliges and walks out of David's office.

At The Protest

Uriah was placed on the frontline of the protest with a bull horn in his hand. As, he marched the soldiers with him held up signs that had the names of individuals who were slain senselessly. The names were as follows: Emmett Till, Breonna Taylor, George Floyd, Trevon Martin, Michael Brown etc.

"We won't be oppressed any longer! We won't be enslaved in our minds! We will be everything that we are called to be! The victory is ours! We will prosper and move forward to take what rightfully belongs to us! You can try to stop us but we will succeed by any means necessary!" Uriah passionately screams through his bull horn.

The soldiers who were with Uriah were amped up, began to shout loudly as well as pump their fists and signs in the air. As the army was moving forward a bullet hit Uriah in his heart, and he fell face forward onto the ground. The soldiers trampled over Uriah's body as they moved forward to conquer the territory.

Chapter 16

Create In Me A Clean Heart

"If we confess our sins, He is faithful and just to forgive us our sins and to cleanse us from all unrighteousness." -1 John 1:9

Bathsheba's House

Eve is consoling Bathsheba as she cries uncontrollably with a runny nose and continuous drooling.

"It's my fault. It's all my fault. I should have supported him more and not been so selfish about my own desires. I wish I would have listened to you, then Uri would still be here. Why did I decide to act out of loneliness? I shouldn't have been striving for attention and bathing publicly just because I wanted to be seen. My personal issues killed my husband, and he didn't deserve it. He was such a good man," she yells hysterically while crying and holding her stomach.

"Sheba, it's not only your fault, and you shouldn't be too hard on yourself. Yeah, if I am being honest you did play a major role in all of this, but Uriah did as well," Eve adamantly tells Bathsheba the truth.

"Eve, I wish the outcome were different, and I wasn't the cause of his death. How could I do such a thing?!" she cries while wiping her eyes, blowing her nose, and rocking back and forth.

Eve grabs Bathsheba by the hand, holds her face, and makes Bathsheba lift up her head to look at her.

"Sheba, sweetheart! We all sin and fall short of the glory of God. Yeah, if I keep it real with you God saw everything that you were doing. Nothing and I mean nothing you do can ever separate you from His love. Although you didn't feel loved and felt lonely doesn't make it okay to seek attention from other men and to step out on your man. God can fill all of your voids like no other and He cares for you so much, Sheba. Repent and turn from your sin. Tell God that you are sorry from your heart. We have to deal with the repercussions of our choices by owning our mess. Nevertheless, we don't need to live in guilt and shame after we repent and turn from our wrongdoings. Trust me, God still has great plans for you and loves you very much, Sheba. He is a forgiving, graceful and merciful God. I have to get back to the restaurant now, but call me if you need anything," Eve encourages while looking into Bathsheba's sad, puffy eyes.

Bathsheba and Eve walk to the door, hug tightly and Bathsheba closes the door behind Eve. Bathsheba begins to cry with her back up against the closed door.

Eden's Restaurant

Marvin Sapp is ministering *Grace and Mercy* at the restaurant.

Bathsheba's House

Bathsheba gets down on her knees, prays and repent for her sins. *Grace and Mercy* is playing.

"God please forgive me. I am sorry for all of the wrong I have done. I am sorry for committing adultery and trying to fill voids myself instead of allowing you to do it. I am sooo sorry for mistreating my husband. I am sooo sorry. I wish I could take it back. Please forgive me," she cries sincerely and prays slowly and meaningfully.

Correctional Facility

The ladies are in silent awe that Bathsheba and Uriah's relationship ended with such a deadly twist.

"Dang poor Uriah. He didn't even deserve to go out like that. He was set up for no reason of his own. He was a real good dude," Cassandra says in disbelief shaking her head.

"Naw, Uriah, should not have been treating Ol' girl like that neither. She all bathing in the nude for others to see her. Who knows maybe she didn't have a freak 'em dress. I don't even know, but I do know Uriah should have been taking care of home. Then, David would not have had the opportunity to put it on Bathsheba," Niecy passionately defends with enlarged eyes.

Niecy and Cassandra bicker back in forth dramatically as they represent Uriah and Bathsheba's cases.

"You both made some compelling arguments. Although, David and Bathsheba sinned greatly God punished them, forgave, and blessed them. In fact, David is still identified as being a man after God's own heart despite his failures. God's anger lasts for only a moment, but His favor lasts for a lifetime. Thank you, God!" she says with conviction lifting up her hand and praising God.

"Sometimes, Mrs. Deborah starts getting all happy up in here. I just love her," Niecy whispers to Cassandra as she stares and grins at Deborah.

"Oh, you know what? I didn't share with you that David and Bathsheba ended up getting married. Their first child died but afterwards God blessed them with a son named Solomon. Their son is noted for being the wisest man that has ever lived. So even when we make poor decisions, God will forgive us when we repent and will still bless us," Deborah states with a huge smile on her face.

The ladies are so engaged with Deborah's storytelling and doses of encouragement.

"Mrs. Deborah, I know you have another story to tell us. Don't leave us hanging like that," Cassandra petitions while holding her hand out.

Chapter 17

I Ain't Ready

"O daughters of Jerusalem, I adjure you by the gazelles and the does of the field; Do not arouse or awaken love until the time is right." Song of Solomon 3:5- Berean Study Bible

"Hmmm, let me see. I told you David and Bathsheba had gotten married. Ok! I do…I did!" she assures after contemplating with her fist on her chin.

The grateful inmates lean forward in their chairs and give Deborah their full attention.

"Back in the day, there was a lady from Southeast, D.C., who was absolutely breathtaking. Whenever, she walked into a room she became the room y'all. The attention was always on Wella, a golden brown petite stunning sistah. It was just something about Wella to which the men were drawn," she says with an entertaining theatrical tone and hand movements.

Wella's House

The melodious sound of Keyondra Lockett's *Real Love* is playing while six brides wearing white wedding gowns and grooms dressed in suits with bow ties are exchanging nuptials at different locations. Then, Wella walks down the aisle in a beautiful black wedding dress with a long train to meet her groom. Wella's groom lifts up her veil then the phone rings right before Wella determines the groom's identity. Wella wakes up from her dream, sits up making a loud sound of frustration. She beats on her pillow to release her disappointment. Wella gives her lover the side eye while he talks on the phone. Tyrone, Wella's lover is a scrumptious pecan brown with a sculpted physique and beautiful brown eyes.

"Hello! Sure. No problem! Good night," Tyrone states in a deep and tired voice.

"Well, what does she want this time and at this wee hour in the morning? " she asks agitatedly while lying with her elbow dug into the pillow and her head resting on her hand as she eyeballs Tyrone.

"Well, you know my wife and I have a child together. She was calling to let me know that she needs me to take our daughter to school in the morning, because she has a conflicting appointment. She forgot to tell me earlier," he states while yawning and laying his head comfortably on his pillow closing his eyes.

"So you're telling me that your wife had to call to inform you of what she needed from you at 2:00 a.m. in the morning? Naw, that is just plain disrespectful. She has her nerve. I just can't, 'cause she is truly trying it! We have been living together for three whole months now. Again, when will the divorce be finalized? Your wife…. I hate when you say that. You have this whole thing, we call ourselves doing here twisted," she states with a stank attitude while shaking her head.

"Come on, baby. Now, don't be that way. I will be divorced before you can say I do. I am just playing. I will be divorced really soon. You know you are the only one that I want, and that is why I am here with you at 2:00 a.m. in the mornin'. Now, get some sleep, woman, unless you want to do that thing I like," he states while gently kissing her on various parts of her upper body.

"Hmmm. If you insist, I think I will do that thing you like," she smirks as she stares into his eyes and kisses him tenderly while straddling him.

They begin to kiss each other intimately pulling the sheets over their bodies.

The next morning at Wella's house, Tyrone is putting on his clothes rushing to get out of the door to take his daughter to school. Wella is still in the bed smirking with the sheets covering her nude body.

"I have to hurry and get out of here so that my daughter will be on time for school. How could you let me oversleep like that," he asks angrily while pulling up his pants.

"Well, you were the one who insisted I do that thing that you like," she states and giggles.

"I don't have time for your jokes right now. I have to make sure that my daughter goes to school on time. This is a serious issue," he states angrily as he puts his shirt on over his head.

"Cool! Do what you need to do for you, but I probably won't be here when you get back. Today is the day that I am leaving for my girls trip. Don't have any girls in my house, and I am not joking," she says seriously and begins packing her things.

"I guess I'll see you when you get back. Have a good time! Who's all going on this trip with you?" he asks while kissing her on her cheek before walking out the door.

"My girls! You know, the ones who don't judge me," she states while packing pairs of shoes to match each outfit perfectly.

Walking back and forth from the bedroom to the bathroom, Wella grabs her toiletries from the bathroom to add to her suitcase. She stops packing to look at herself in the mirror momentarily.

"You know Rahab, almond brown with body for days who's always the life of the party; Gomer, petite cinnamon brown with the cute booty; and Mary, mocha brown with long hair and that killer bod -my ride or dies," she states louder to make sure that Tyrone hears her in the other room.

The girls are at the door when Tyrone opens it up to leave. He waves and rushes out the door. The girls greet each other, hug, and exchange smooches.

"You are always late and you need to work on that," Gomer says as she smiles and hugs Wella while walking through the door.

"Gomer, I came on my cycle… this month," Wella responds while rolling her eyes.

The girls fall out laughing as they hug each other.

"You always have something slick to say," Gomer laughs shaking her head.

"Well, I'm ready now. Eve wants us to stop by before we leave. She wants us to listen to her act that is performing this upcoming Sunday at her Gospel Brunch," she says as they all walk out of the door.

Chapter 18

Help A Sistah Out

"Where there is no guidance, the people falls, but in an abundance of counselors there is safety."
-Proverbs 11:14 ESV

Eve's Garden Restaurant

The ladies walk into Eve's restaurant, and they all run up to Eve and hug her tenderly. Eve smiles and is happy to see the ladies.

"Thanks for coming. Order what you like! These meals are on me. So, tell me, what have you ladies been up to lately?" she asks while putting her elbow on the bar her fist resting on her chin.

"You don't have to tell me twice. I don't even have to look at the menu. I would like the wholegrain angel hair pasta with your home-made tomato sauce as well as the recipe please," Rahab states with her hands in prayer posture.

"Now, if tell you, you can't give my recipe out," she says pointing at Rahab.

"Now, you know how I do. I ain't telling a soul. I will hide it and take it my grave," Rahab says with a straight face.

They all laugh.

"For real First Lady, I want you to give me the recipe. To answer question from earlier, I have been just taking care of my man and my family. Boaz is growing up so fast on me," she smiles enjoying the restaurant's ambience.

"Same here Ray. I have been taking care of my babies and giving Hosea all this good loving. I just love that man," Gomer says while rubbing her hands down the silhouette of her shape.

Eve chuckles, "I ain't mad at y'all. How about you Mary and Wella?" Eve inquires with a grin.

"Firstly, I can't eat right now because I don't eat until after 12:00 p.m.," she retorts while looking at the menu.

"Well, you surely are going to make sure you take some of my good cooking with you. Eat it on the road," she insists staring at Mary intently.

"Yes, mam! I have been working on improving my financial portfolio with Martha and Lazarus and I have been traveling on the Good News Tour" she says sipping on a glass of wine.

"I see you big baller, shot caller. Well, you know I have been doing the same ol' thing. Maybe you can help a sistah out. I have been having this dream consistently, but I always wake up before the dream is finished", she contemplates as she looks at the stage.

A beautiful woman by the name of Chante Moore graces the stage and with all eyes on her she begins to sing *Jesus, I Need You*.

"I absolutely love this song. The lyrics are so real," Mary confesses and praises as Chante sings.

The ladies begin to converse and listen to Chante sing as the music plays.

"So, tell us about your dream, because your energy seemed a little off ever since you walked in here," Eve recognizes and looks with concern with one eyebrow raised at Wella.

The ladies turn their attention to Wella as she proceeds to tell her dream.

"I know, Mrs. Eve, but this dream has truly been bothering me. I continuously see six couples getting married. Then, I am walking down the aisle to meet my groom in this bad wedding dress with a gorgeous veil. As my groom begins to lift my veil, I wake up. I don't know who the groom is," she states while frustratedly banging her fist on the bar.

"Well, we know this bar here is not your husband so you can stop banging it," she says seriously while gently rubbing Wella's hands.

All the ladies including Eve began to laugh.

"Wella, you know I am just playing with you. It sounds like God is trying to tell you something because you keep having the dream repeatedly. I don't know what it means though. Pray and ask God what it means. When God tells you the meaning of your dream, pay attention to what He is saying and do exactly what He is telling you to do. Trust and know that He loves you and cares for you more than you can ever fathom. He's not a man that shall lie. He loves you so much Wella," Eve states warmly as she hugs the back of Wella's neck.

Rahab, Gomer, and Mary agree that Eve gives Wella great advice. They begin to lift their hands and praise God while enjoying Chante sing. They give her a standing ovation when she finishes. Chante bows and blows kisses at the ladies.

"Thanks, Evie Eve! Chante is a keeper. The food was delicious as always, but we have to get on the road. I want to go on a hike today before it gets too late," Wella states as she chews the last bite of her food and sips her drink.

"It's my pleasure to feed you and spend time with you all. Thanks for stopping by," she smiles with joy.

All the ladies thank and hug Eve as they leave the restaurant.

Chapter 19

A Spoonful of Medicine

*"A merry heart does good, like medicine,
But a broken spirit dries up the bones."
-Proverbs 17:22 NKJV*

Car Ride

The ladies were in Mary's four-door white Ferrari traveling to the country club for the girls' getaway. Rahab and Gomer were in the front of the car, and Mary and Wella were sitting in the back.

"So, Wella do you have any clue what this dream you keep having may mean?" Gomer inquires as she takes an air pod out of her ear.

"Yeah, because your panties are caught up in a bunch." Rahab laughs and then taps Gomer on her knee.

Mary laughs and shakes her head at Rahab's comment, "Girl, sometimes you just don't know what to say up out of your mouth."

"Well, you know I am just speaking the truth. This dream has taking her for a loop," Rahab states boldly with a sassy attitude while holding her hand out.

"Ray, you're right! I keep thinking about this dream over and over again. I think the five weddings represent five of the men that I've dated. All of them were married," she ponders as she enjoys nature's scenery from the window.

The ladies were completely silent for a few minutes as they listened to the radio.

"Bowlegged, caramel brown Franklin, of course, was older and my first love. He showed this young chic here from the hood how to run game. He was a rich businessman dealing in street pharmaceuticals," Wella explains as she reminisces on her time spent with Franklin.

"You mean fine Franklin ran all the corners in the neighborhood and had some other businesses as well," Rahab interrupts anxious to get her point across.

"Yep, he made me feel so special. He bought me the latest designer fashions and took me to the best restaurants. I loved going to Chinatown late at night," Wella smiled as she contemplated on her late night excursions with Franklin.

"Why did you go out to eat late at night, Wella?" Mary asks to start confrontation already knowing the answer to the question.

"Because his wife was sleep and he was handling his business," Gomer comments and cries laughing uncontrollably.

They all laugh.

"Yep, his wife knew about us along. She didn't care as long as Frank took care of her, the kids, and their luxurious lifestyle. She was good," Wella explains to clear the air.

"Dang, Frank was like that? I am shocked I didn't come across him first," Gomer ponders with her hand on her chin.

"Naw, that one was mine, G," Wella reinforces to shut Gomer's comment down.

"And his wife's," Rahab coughs intentionally under her breath.

They crack up laughing.

"Y'all can say what y'all want but he bought me my first apartment and car. I was young and the life he introduced me to was so exciting. He helped groom me into who I am today. He showed me how to dress, speak articulately and how to not be a product of my environment. Frank paid for my college and showed me the finer things in life," Wella gratefully explains as she raises her voice over the other ladies.

"What happened to you and Frank?" Rahab asks as she turns her head and eyes slightly to the direction of the backseat.

"Frank went to jail on King Pin charges and may never get out unless he snitches," Wella shares while scrolling through her cell phone.

"I don't know if it's true or not but I heard snitches get stitches. I'm just saying it's just what I heard. Don't shoot the messenger," Rahab smiles and puts her hands up as she slightly directs her attention towards the backseat.

"Yes, we remember how much you loved yourself some Frank, but what was that tall guy's name who played basketball? He wasn't from the DMV, but whenever he was in town, he went to Berry Farms to play in their night tournaments. You know who I am talking about. Stop acting like you don't know who I am talking about. You and Gomer would be out there late at night getting a contact from all that weed they were smoking," are questions anxiously looking through the rear-view mirror as she drives.

"Dante!" Wella and Gomer yell Dante's name at the same time.

Wella smiles and remembers, "Dante was so tall with that yummy tootsie roll complexion. Yes, he surely satisfied my sweet tooth."

They fall out laughing and high five each other.

"That's the guy you were with when TMZ was the first to report his infidelity," Rahab cries laughing.

They all laugh!

"Girrrl, yes! I was so embarrassed that I ended up putting a long weave in my hair, because my hair was short when the story was reported. I wore shades and a baseball cap for about a month until the story died down. Girl, that brings back so many memories," Wella chuckles as she tells the story shaking her head.

"Whatever happened to that pastor you were messing around wit'? He was married and had some lil' PKs running around. He was fine and all but you lost me when he was coming over your house to lay his hands and to get your offerings. Hallelujah!" Gomer blurts out, as she bows her head and raises her hands to pray.

The ladies all fall out laughing.

"Pastor Washington's gray hair and his belly's circumference from eating all those chicken dinners and Friday night Fish Frys turned a sistah on! Pastor Washington's sermons were sooo good," she states as she looks out the car window.

Rahab adds, "You were going around sayin', 'Issa First Lady now,' and I said, "Naw First Ho is more like it," she cries laughing.

They all fell out.

"Ray, now you got your nerve, but I'm going to give that one to you. You know who really was a sweet guy?" Wella asks pleasantly.

"Who, the mail man?!" Mary blurts out while raising her hands.

"We love you but also love giving you a hard time. So, you said there were six couples getting married in the dream", Rahab inquires with care as she looks out the as she texts on her cellphone.

"Yep, there were six couples altogether getting hitched. The sweet guy I just mentioned was Martin. He had a dream that one day he would own his own record label where little black boys and girls would come together and make music. His dream came true and he is a billionaire now. I had free tickets and VIP access to all his artists' shows. He was so humble and taught me so much about business and seizing the right opportunities. Out of all the guys that I have dated, I believe we would have had a wonderful relationship if he wasn't married. He was unhappy sexually with his wife, so I was faithful to perform to his liking. I was just making the best use of my skills and talents. His wife was straight bougie and thought she was better than everybody who wasn't raised with a silver spoon in their mouth. She thought she was better than me and I couldn't stand it," Wella states emotionally as she reads the text that chimes on her phone.

"Wella, you will always be My First Ho, Love Pastor Washington," Rahab texts all the ladies.

Wella reads Rahab's text aloud and all the ladies laugh.

Chapter 20

Don't Judge Me

"A friend loves at all times, and a brother is born for a time of adversity." -Proverbs 17:17 NIV

Country Club

The ladies walk into the beautiful country club lobby with contemporary décor and see the upper-class elites walking to and fro. While the ladies are waiting near the concierge area, a woman and her friends walk up to Wella.

"Lookie, lookie here. Phee-Phii-Phoo-Phuum, I smell a hood rat," the lady states as she walks around Wella slowly.

"This is something else. I was just talking about you," Wella responds with a confident smirk on her face and her right eyebrow raised.

"What are you doing here? You don't belong here, because this is truly out of your league," the lady states in an uppity tone as she sips her wine.

"Oh, so you're still salty about Martin. I see. Well, I can't help if my milkshake brought Martin to the yard, and he likes it better than yours. It's not my problem if you can't please him, but what I will do for you is give you and your girls a discount at my HTTCOYM School. I will also throw in some buddy passes for your gals," she smiles leaning in and whispering to the lady.

"What is the HTTCOYM School?" she inquires in a sididdy fashion.

"It stands for "How To Take Care of Your Man." By the way, Martin believes I belong here now get the hell out of my face," she raises her voice as she pulls down her shades from her eyes to her nose.

Wella, Gomer, Rahab and Mary walk away and enter the elevator as the lady and her friends watch.

"Oh, and take the silver spoon out of your mouths," Gomer yells as she sucks on her lollipop.

The elevator door shuts while the lady and her friends look with their mouths open in disgust. Wella, Rahab, Gomer and Mary laugh hysterically. The ladies reach the upper penthouse suite and exit the elevator. Mary puts her finger up to her lips while laughing to quiet the ladies down. They were in awe of the spacious suite that featured big windows to showcase natural lighting. Each woman had her own room with its own personal bathroom.

"So, what do you think?" Mary asks with her hands held wide open with a closed lip smile.

The ladies all smile and simultaneously express, "We love it!"

"It's nothing but the best for my girls," she smiles and sips on her Essentia water.

"The scenery is beautiful and tranquil here. It's so peaceful and despite the pigeons in the lobby....it's perfect." Rahab states while staring out one of the huge windows.

Wella had been quiet ever since she entered the penthouse. Gomer nudged Wella with her elbow inconspicuously.

"Hey, are you alright? You have been less talkative since you seen that chic in the lobby. She didn't get to you did she?" Gomer whispers in Wella's ear.

"Wella smacks her lips together and responds, "Girl, please! I am so used to being insulted as well as the talk of the town. Now, it just rolls right off my back when it happens," Wella sternly responds as she stands up from her seat.

Wella goes to the bathroom and takes an honest look at herself in the mirror. She put her hands down on the sink and moves close to the mirror to wipe the tears from her eyes. She walks out of the bathroom and *Waiting to Exhale* is playing on the mounted flatscreen TV.

"They remind me so much of us because of their bond. They were there to encourage one another during various seasons of their lives," Mary eloquently states as she quenches her thirst with more water.

"Do you remember how we met?" she laughs as she walks to sit down on the couch.

The all laugh as they recall their initial bonding moments. The ladies each take turns telling their most memorable portions of the story of when they first met.

"We were at Gabriella's Restaurant, before it was Eve's Restaurant. Chuck Brown was in the house, and it was packed. We were all at the bar but didn't know each other personally yet," Rahab remembers excitedly.

They were all laughing.

"Wella was sporting her drop socks and high top Reebok's that that fine hustler, Rick, bought her. It was Rick's wife that brought us all together. She was standing on the other side of the bar across from us. We named Rick, Slick Rick after that night because every time his wife would turn away he would blow a kiss at Wella behind his wife's back," Gomer cries laughing while demonstrating Slick Rick's foulness.

They were all laughing uncontrollably.

"It was absolutely hilarious when his wife caught him…She looked at Wella," Mary explains while giggling and smacking her knee.

Wella, Rahab, Gomer, and Mary yell in unity, "Ho you gonna sit up here and disrespect me in my face like that?!"

They all fell out laughing.

"Who you calling a Ho?! Me?!" Mary points to herself and asks with a 'bout it 'bout it look.

"I think she's talking about me," Rahab dramatically blurts out with one hand on her hip.

"Nah, she must be talking about me….cause I goes hard," Gomer replies as she points to herself.

"No, she is talking about me because her husband has a thing for me," Wella laughs loudly and stops after one chuckle.

"He has a thing for me too," Rahab giggles and licks her lips slowly.

"And me too," Gomer adds as she pushes her cleavage up noticeably leaning over.

"I was just with Slick Rick before they came up in here. I wasn't playing 'cause I didn't know which one of us hoes this chic was talking about. I might not know you personally, but I have heard of all y'all track records. You know how the streets talk. This round of drinks is on me. Here's to the Hoes!" Mary laughs as she puts her drink in the air and nods her head.

They all clank their glasses together and yell, "Cheers...To...The...Hoes!!" Slick Rick's wife nastily grits on the ladies and quickly stomps out the bar livid. The ladies introduce themselves and continue to talk.

"Do y'all smoke? If y'all do follow me," Mary says as she stands up and pushes in her bar stool.

They all stand up, push in their bar stools, and follow Mary upstairs to the rooftop. They sit on the ground with their backs to the wall of the building. They bond over a joint as they look at the scenery of the city.

"I come up here sometimes to calm my nerves and think about life. So, tell me honestly, if what I hear on the streets is true, why do you do the things that you do?" Mary asks while inhaling the smoke through her nose.

"Mary Jane, Mary Jane is calling my name! I do what is best for me, because it's about me," Gomer professes honestly with her eyes closed and head bent down as she enjoys her high.

"I am just your typical around the way girl that looks out for my brothers, and I love the benefits. It's truly rewarding for me," Rahab states while puffing the joint and twirling her hair.

"I just take what I want when I want it as long as it works for me. How about you, Mary?" Wella asks with smoke in her mouth as she passes the joint back to Rahab.

"I didn't grow up in these parts, but I am attracted to what it offers…. Especially hugs from these fine thugs. That's my weakness. I'm just sayin," Mary emphasizes as she exhales the smoke through her nose.

They all laugh and agree that there is something about them hugs from them fine thugs as they reminisce on how they met. As they continue to talk while watching *Waiting to Exhale*. Wella's phone rings. She checks her caller ID and notices that it is a call from one of her girlfriends. In fact, she notices that she has several missed calls from her friend. Wella returns her friend, Andrea's call.

"Hey, girl," Andrea greets in a low tone.

"Hey, Andrea," Wella smiles as she hears the voice of her girl.

"Have you heard about Ali?" Andrea asks hesitantly.

"No, what's going on?" Wella inquires anxiously while bracing herself for the news.

"I apologize for being the bearer of bad news ….but Ali passed away. It's all over social media and my friend confirmed it with his family. I am sorry Wella. I know how much he meant to you," she states empathetically.

Wella hangs up the phone without saying goodbye. She turns around to Rahab, Mary, and Gomer with a look of shock on her face. The ladies are concerned about Wella because she was speechless.

"Wella are you ok?" Gomer asks while putting her arm around her.

"He's gone. Ali is gone," Wella announces softly.

"What do you mean he's gone?" Mary asks for clarification.

"Do you mean like not dealing with you anymore or like...?" Rahab asks in a seriously foolish manner.

Rahab acts like she is slitting her throat with a knife, and then croaks on the couch. The girls look at Rahab in disbelief.

"Ray, sometimes you are just sooo extra. Now, isn't the time," Mary informs Rahab with tight jaws to keep from laughing.

"I am sorry, boo! I just thought he decided not to deal with you anymore because of his beautiful wife," Rahab blurts out and clears her throat while stroking Wella's hand.

Wella snatches her hand back from Rahab and grits.

"Ali died last night!" she raises her shaky voice as tears flow from her eyes.

The ladies gather closely around Wella and hug her tightly.

"He was a good dude. He was so sweet and kind to you," Gomer says compassionately while stroking Wella's hair.

Rahab interjects while rubbing her hands together and looking away from the ladies, "Dang, I know his wife and kids are set…..for life! I'm jus' sayin!"

Everybody looks at Rahab in amazement.

"Ray…. You stupid," Mary acknowledges with a straight face.

Wella smirks and raises her voice in an agitated tone, "No, all of you are right and yep…. Ray is stupid! For real though, Ali was such a good man who saw and appreciated me for me. Maybe, it had something to do with him being older which made him more mature. Or maybe, his momma just raised him right. He was a gentleman, indeed. He saw my potential and wanted to help bring out the best in me."

"Physically or sexually?" Rahab asks with her hand held in the form of a microphone directed at Wella.

"Please get her before I do! I met him when I was considering plastic surgery. Not only was he a doctor that never forgot where he came from, Ali went back to help people in his community. We would travel often to Africa and Haiti where he would give medical treatment to those in need. And, yes I assisted him in helping his patients. Whenever, I went to these countries I was totally accepted, and I felt so free. The only reason we stopped seeing each other was because his wife found out about us. She gave him an ultimatum. She told him that he better leave me alone or she was going to take him for everything that he owned. Needless to say, he chose her," she reminisces on the memorable times as she wipes her tears.

"I am sooo sorry for your loss, Sis. I am here if you need anything. Please just let me know," Mary states sincerely while hugging Wella.

"I am here for you, too," she concurs and hugs Wella along with Mary.

"Me, too Wella! I am just trying to make my sister laugh instead of cry," Rahab states in a heartfelt manner as she hugs Wella.

"I am going to retire for the evening so I can get a good night's sleep. I love you all too and thanks for always being there for me," she somberly conveys as she walks into her room.

Chapter 21

You Must Not Know About Me

> "But whoever drinks of the water that I will give him will never be thirsty again. The water that I will give him will become in him a spring of water welling up to eternal life." -John 4:14 ESV

Wella looks in the bathroom mirror and sighs. She gets in the bed and puts the covers over her head and cries quietly. Later that night, she has the same dream once again but wakes up during the same part of the dream without seeing the face of the man who lifts her veil. Wella drinks a bottle of water beside her bed to quench her thirst. The next morning before the rest of the ladies get up and while most people are sleeping, Wella decides to take a solo run on the trail to get some fresh air and enjoy the scenery.

Refreshing Reservoir

Wella sees a reservoir that contains fresh spring water and enjoys the serene solitude of peace and quiet. As Wella, digs in her bag for a water bottle to fill with refreshing spring water, a man comes up to her.

"Can you give me a drink of water?" a handsome man with a gentle spirit asks politely.

"Why is you asking me for a drink and even talking to a chic like me. Man, you don't come from where I come from and your people don't deal with my people. So, man, what do you really want? she inquires suspiciously and with a slight attitude.

"*If only you knew*, he sang then said, the gift of God who is standing here in front of you and is asking you for a drink. You would have asked me for a drink, and I would have given you living water," the man confidently states with swag.

Wella begins to cry laughing while looking at the man, "Oh my goshhhhh, living water. I would have asked you for living water. You are absolutely hilarious. I have never heard that one before. That is a smooth line. Ok, I get it chivalry isn't dead. Woo!"

Wella is still regaining her composure from laughing so hard.

"If I was going to decide to get you a drink of water, how were you going to get it? How was you going to get this living water you were talking about. Ewww, I don't know you like that to give you my bottle and then drink after you. I'm just saying! I don't play them type of games," Wella informs in a sassy manner while laughing.

"If you drink this water in which you are drawing you will still be thirsty after you drink it, but if you drink the water that I give you, you will never thirst again. The water I give you will become a fountain of water springing up into everlasting life. I'm just sayin," the man said with more swag than the first time while nodding his head.

Wella has a flashback of waking up from her dream when she drinks a bottle of water to quench her thirst.

"Sir, give me this water that you're talking about. I don't want to thirst again," she responds humbly.

"Go tell your husband to come here," the man commanded.

Wella's eyes began to tear up as she speaks in a lowly manner, "I don't have a husband."

"So, you say you don't have a husband but in fact you have had five husbands. Even the one you are with now is not your husband. So, you have spoken truthfully when you say you don't have a husband," he explains looking intently into her eyes and through her soul.

Wella sits down by the water with her hands on her knees and tears slowly run down her face.

"I know what happened to you when you were 10 years old. Your father cheated on your mother and left you and your mother for that other woman. Their divorce as well as the grief your mother endured left you numb, broken and bitter. You made a vow to yourself that you wouldn't be hurt by a man, like your mom experienced, but preferred to take on the role of the other woman. In your mind, you believe the other woman has the power and control she desires," the man states compassionately while sharing Wella's past.

"Are you a prophet or something? How do you know about me and my life?" she asks timidly wiping away tears with her shirt.

"Wella, you worship what you do not know. See, God is Spirit and you, beloved, must worship in spirit and truth," the man speaks the truth compassionately while sitting next to Wella their by the reservoir.

"I have heard that when the Messiah comes He will tell us all things," she smiles as though a weight has been lifted off of her countenance.

"I am He," the man smiles while wiping her tears and looking Wella in her eyes.

The man's brothers came to meet him and Wella smiles, mouths with her lips thank you and runs back energetically to the country club to meet her friends. When Wella arrives she catches the next elevator and begins to sing *Jesus I Want You,* the same song that she heard at Eve's restaurant. Nevertheless, Wella is not alone in the elevator as she anticipates. Martin's wife is in the elevator's corner shaking her head.

"You are such a heathen. Have you taken a good look at yourself in the mirror lately? You go around hurting other women who have done nothing wrong to you, Wella. You are a home wrecker. You're sleeping with my husband and then have the audacity to come up in here singing about Jesus. Give me a break! Do you even know Him or have a relationship with Him, because if you did you wouldn't go around hurting people intentionally like you are doing," the lady breaks down and cries as she laments.

"Dang, it is so true that when you come off of a mountaintop experience the enemy really tries to come at you hard! Let me get something straight with you. I am not sleeping with Martin anymore. I stopped in 2019 or maybe it was 2020. I can't remember. I really do need Jesus though, and I met Him today. Before today, I didn't have a relationship with Him, and I am going to change my ways. This is new for me so please bear with me. I am sorry for any pain that I have caused you. You didn't deserve it. Please except my apology," Wella delicately expresses regret as she puts her hands in prayer posture.

The lady wipes her tears and states, "I will forgive you as long as you give me free classes at your HTTCOYM school."

The elevator door opens to the lady's floor and Wella presses the button to hold the door open.

Wella laughs and smiles, "We have a deal!"

Wella skips into her room and finds Rahab, Mary and Gomer lounging around.

"Good morning, Chicas," Wella yells joyfully with bright eyes.

Wella hopped on Rahab and everybody starts looking at Wella.

"What has gotten into you?" Rahab asks Wella with a look of confusion.

Rahab pushes Wella off of her, and Wella plops down on to the seat next to Rahab.

"I meet a man and when I say I meet a man I mean The Man," Wella recalls grinning ear to ear.

Tears stream down Wella's, face and Rahab taps Wella on the shoulder.

"You mean you meet a white man. I didn't know you were into the swirl thing," Rahab utters in a low tone.

"Naw buddy, it's written all over your face and you are glowing, Love. There is only one who can make you smile, and then cry in a matter of seconds just like you did. Tell us all about it," Mary insists excitedly wanting to hear Wella's story.

Wella tells her friends all the details about her encounter with The Man. They embrace Wella and celebrate this momentous occasion.

"If I am going to start my new life off right, I have to handle something really quickly," Wella states adamantly while walking over to her bag.

Wella grabs her phone.

"I think I better call Tyrone," she states without a smile her head tilted to the left.

"*Call him*," Rahab, Gomer and Mary sang melodiously.

Wella tells Siri to call Tyrone. Tyrone is at Wella's house watching a sports match as he answers the phone.

"Hey, Babe! I was just thinking about you," Tyrone happily expresses as he lowers the TV volume to hear Wella clearly.

"Tyrone, I was just thinking about you too, and how you need to get all your stuff out of my house. We are done! Go back home to your wife," Wella screams loudly as she mugs at the phone.

Wella hangs up the phone while Tyrone is still trying to grasp the fact he is getting kicked out of Wella's house.

Rahab, Gomer, and Mary hug Wella and tell her repeatedly how proud they are of her. The ladies put on their clothes and decide to go downstairs for brunch.

"When I gave my life to Christ it was the best decision that I made, but I guess others who knew me prior kept bringing up my past. That used to make me so mad at first, but it doesn't bother me now. I definitely know who I am and that I am not what I used to be," Mary confidently shares with a smirk and raised shoulders.

"It used to bother me as well, because I expected people that I offended in the past to show mercy. When we sin, we are supposed to ask God for forgiveness as well as the person we offended. Unfortunately, some people will never allow you to forget your past, forgive you and will just keep bringing that mess up. I am good now though. I know God forgives me and people don't have a heaven nor a hell to put me in," Gomer clearly explains while swerving her head.

"Well-er-ra... I never gave a flying... Hold up, let me start over again. I never gave a...hmmm, let me see if I can put this in laymen terms. Ok, ok let me give this another try. I have never really cared what people had to say about me, because I'm a G," Rahab states while mugging her face.

The ladies laugh at Rahab.

"Yeah, I hear you. I believe others won't allow you to forget your past, nor forgive your offenses depending on what's in their hearts," Wella agrees and raises her eyebrows.

The ladies wait in the lobby for their table to be ready, and Martin's wife and her friends walk by them. Wella and Martin's wife wink at each other, smile and nod their heads. Gomer rolls her neck in shock and looks at Wella strangely.

"What was that about?" Gomer inquires confused.

"Oh nothing," Wella states and smiles as she treasures their elevator conversation in her heart.

When Wella goes to bed that night she has the same recurring dream, but this time in the dream the wedding dress that she's wearing is white. Also, when the man lifts up her veil, the man is Jesus. Wella said yes, I do and enters into an eternal relationship with The Man who is the love of her life.

Correctional Facility

"Wella was delivered, set free and made whole just like that. It only takes one encounter with Jesus to turn your entire life around," Deborah confidently speaks as she scans the room, points her finger and looks each inmate in her eyes.

"So, you ain't bluffing us are you? So, you telling me there is a woman named Wella in the Bible who was going hard like that", Cassandra inquires leaning forward in her seat.

"She was definitely going hard like that as you say, but she is referred to as the woman at the well or as the

Samaritan woman at the well in the book of John 4:4-26 in the Bible," Deborah clarifies smiling.

"Hmmm," Cassandra sighs and leans back in her chair with her arms folded.

"Well, I have my last and final story to share with you," Deborah informs as she brightly smiles and rubs her hands together.

Chapter 22

Saved By the Bell

"Since, therefore, we have now been justified by his blood, much more shall we be saved by him from the wrath of God." -Romans 5:9 ESV

Shopping Mall

After brunch, the ladies decide to go to a nearby shopping mall to pick up a few items.

"Ever since my encounter with The Man, I feel like a burden has truly been lifted off of me," Wella states joyously.

"Girl, yessss! I know exactly what you mean! I felt the same way and still do today. My life is truly changed for the better. Now, I am not saying that I don't have challenges and obstacles, but I can just hand all of it right over to Jesus. He changed my life," Mary agrees and shares the moment.

The ladies walk into the store and notice a beautiful dress with a red ribbon. Rahab takes the dress off the rack and asks the salesperson the cost of the dress. The salesperson is a thin fashionable woman with a short blonde haircut draped in couture.

"This is a one of a kind designer original. This dress will look simply gorgeous on you. In fact, I believe it was tailored and made just for you," the salesperson describes with a twinkle in her eye.

"I see…spoken just like an experienced salesperson. Well, I do agree it will look gorgeous on me, darling. How much is it?" Rahab asks holding the dress up to her body as she looks in the mirror.

Gomer, Wella and Mary sit back in comfy chairs in the waiting area and watch the entertaining exchange between Rahab and the salesperson.

"This dress is $75 and remember it is a one of a kind. No one will have it except for you," the salesperson persuades.

"I love this dress…especially this red ribbon. We have a deal if you let it go for $50. I won't tell if you won't tell, since it is tailored and made just for me," Rahab smiles and looks at the salesperson from the corner of her eye in the mirror.

The ladies laugh and shake their heads as this was not unusual behavior for Rahab.

"You drive a hard bargain, but we have a deal. It's nice doing business with you, Fashionista," she smiles as she rings up the dress and hangs it in a bag.

"Likewise, and it takes one to know one," she says as she struts with her new dress out of the store.

The ladies all follow Rahab.

"When you saw that dress, I knew you would be attracted to the red corded ribbon," Gomer expresses to Rahab.

"Don't act like you know me like that, but yes red is indeed my favorite color," Rahab playfully raised her voice at Gomer and laughs.

"So, what's up with the red corded ribbon?" Wella inquires.

"Well, you know back in the day how I was telling you I was making those coins by any means necessary. The parties that I threw were considered the after party, and the who's who of who would be in the house. I'm talking about celebrities, politicians, you name it and anyone who had money was in those joints that I threw.

On this particular night, Suttle Thoughts was playing with Michelle on the mic. Have you ever heard of a brothel or better yet a whorehouse? Well, I ran the Little Whorehouse of D.C. I believe Gomer you used to make a lot of money at those parties as well as selling raisin' cakes amongst other things," Rahab smirks as she runs her hands down her body.

They all laugh.

"You know dang well, I didn't come to any of your parties," Gomer laughs and raises her fist in Rahab's direction.

"Look, this is my story and I am sticking to it. Now, where was I? Let me see. Ok," Rahab expresses adamantly!

Rahab's House

"Now, where was I? Let me see, ok! I was in love with a man who was fine as ever and well respected around the way. His name is surely not worth mentioning. Listen, I would do anything that he wanted, because you know that I am indeed that ride or die chic. We had so many good times together, but he also had a dark side. On the days that were not so good for him, he would take out the pressure he was feeling on me. The straw that broke the camel's back was when he walked up into my place of business with a woman on his arm. I wanted to choke her out, because she knew that the guy she was with was my man. Shucks, we were like a modern day Bee and Jay, but I was kicked to the left. It was quite evident that he wanted the world to know that he was with her. I didn't release a can of whip tail on her because he was the one that was in the wrong. I was so embarrassed because everybody around the way knew that we were an item. He had the audacity to tell me in front of all the people, my click, that it was over. I was literally heart broken. I couldn't believe that he could treat me like that. I was always there for him, and I loved him more than anything in this world. That was one of my problems, because I put him before God. Y'all, I cried like a baby that night when the party was over. Now you know, I wasn't going to allow people to see the broken side of me so I faked my smile for the rest of the night. You know it's true how the Word says that weeping endures for a night but joy comes in the morning. The next couple of weeks, business went on as usual, because I wasn't going to let anything stop me from getting that coin. I also wasn't going to allow a no good man cause me to be bitter. I am so much better than that. You know sometimes God has to remove some things out of our lives before He decides to bless us. Yes, sometimes it hurts, but God know the plans He has for us," declares the LORD, "plans to prosper us and not to harm us, plans to give us hope and a future," Rahab explains passionately.

One day Gomer was working the walls and these two fine me walked in with colored Timberlands on their feet. That's when I peeped that they weren't from the DMV. It wasn't only their style of dress that indicated that they were not from the area, but it was their accent. I could tell that they were from the other side of the tracks.

During this time, the area in which I lived was really bad y'all and full of idolatry and wickedness. There was all sorts of oppression including economic and mental. Jobs were extremely scarce and people were doing what they had to do by any means to make a dollar. The king pins and others who were in high positions of power were successful in their tactics making money at the cost of hurting others. The majority of these men were arrogant and so full of themselves. They paid me well and considered me as their girl, because I catered to their needs and knew how to keep my mouth shut. Word spread around town rapidly about the two men were not from the DMV that came to my party. When it was over, everyone had left my house except for the two guys I was just telling you about.

"Do you know the party ended about two hours ago? Is there anything that I can do for you?" Rahab asks in a seductive tone bending down in front of them to highlight her round behind.

Both men admire Rahab's beautiful assets, but one of the men was more fond of Rahab than the other. Rahab continues to ask the guys questions while flirting with the man who is noticeably attracted to her.

"Word really spreads fast around here, and I know the reason that you are here and so do all the other man who were at the party tonight. I believe that could be one of the reasons why the majority of the guests left so abruptly to spread the word of your arrival. I don't think it is safe for you to leave at this time, so you can stay here for tonight if you desire. Come on and follow me upstairs," Rahab commands as she motions to the man who is the object of her desire to take her hand.

He grabs Rahab's hand and follows her upstairs along with the other man following behind him. Rahab leads them to her attic to hide them for the night. Rahab hears the doorbell ring and goes downstairs quietly to answer her door. Some of the men from the city came back to find out where the two out of town visitors were.

"You sure have some bad timing because you missed them. They left a few hours ago, I believe they were going towards Baltimore. If you leave now and do about 92 mph going north, I believe you can catch them and do what you need to do to stop them," Rahab falsifies in a believable and dramatic performance.

Rahab goes back upstairs into her attic and tells the two men about her discussion with the men who were at her door looking for them.

"Thank you so much for your hospitality and your kindness! You are indeed the hostess with the mostest! To be honest with you, we are here on business to scope out the nature of this entire community. The individuals who were here tonight will no longer be in power, because the big man that I work for is taking over. This entire area will be revitalized which means everything that you see here now must go. This area is under new management and some of the leaders are against the transition that is about to take place. We are moving in and taking over this territory. In other words, it's a war….but we will be victorious. When the man I work for wages war against the enemy, the battle is already won. The men who were after us know my leader's track record and know that their time is coming to an end. They are rightfully fearful and should be. My leader is not the one to play with," the spy explains in detail to Rahab nodding in reassurance and looking rather buff.

"You make it sound so sexy when you say it like that. Hol' up, is this considered gentrification? I want you to escape from my window upstairs, because I don't need nuffin' happening to my new Boo, " she insists looking at the men out of the corner of her eye as she sips on her coffee.

The spies laugh at Rahab.

"Let me see how I can best explain this to you. The leaders in this community are corrupt in their selfish thinking, and their approach to gaining prosperity. Their ways have had a major impact on the community's inhabitants spiritually, mentally, physically, and financially. The man I serve won't allow this oppressive, catastrophic, generational mindset to enslave you or these people anymore. It's been happening long enough and when my leader says it's over he means it's over. A new regime is moving in for the better livelihood of the people," he explains knowledgeably to Rahab.

"So, what does this territorial purging and takeover look like for me and my family? I am not ready to die. I still have so much to do. *I think I found the love of my life,*" she sings and dances in front of the spy that she likes.

"Love, you did and you don't even know it yet. Let me talk to my man for a minute. Please excuse us," he says politely while bowing down with his hands in prayer posture.

The two spies speak privately with hand movements and head nods that Rahab could see from a distance. Rahab attempts to ear hustle but fails miserably. The other spy laughs at Rahab and waves his hand directing her to come and join the conversation.

"We have a proposition to make with you due to the kindness that you have shown to us. There are no ifs, ands and wonderfully crafted butts about it," he says with a huge grin looking at Rahab.

"What, what did I do?" she smiles and sexily says in a baby voice as she twirls her hair and twists her body from side to side.

The spy and Rahab stare intently into each other's eyes. Then, the spy wipes the sweat from his forehead. The other spy taps his man to regain his focus.

He clears his throat and says, "Mmmm, like I said earlier, we have a proposition to make with you. We are still going to take over this community and overthrow its leadership. Unfortunately, there will be a lot of shedding of blood. Nevertheless, your kindness and your protection of us will save your life. You must follow my instructions thoroughly. I want you to tie a red cord on the window from which you want us to escape. This will be a sign that no one is to come to this house and harm you. Do you hear me? I don't need anything happening to my new Boo, either," he affirms holding Rahab's shoulders and looking into her eyes.

"Up close and personal! Just the way I like it. Hol' up! What about my family? What's going to happen to my family?" Rahab panics and paces the floor with one head on her forehead.

"Bae-Be, no need to stress! I got you, and I got them too! Remember, *I think I must have found the love of my life, too*," he says and sings passionately in a calming tone.

"Get a room," the other spy says while making gagging noises and pointing his finger towards his mouth.

"Listen, make sure that you and your family come in this house and stay inside. Do not leave for anything! So, make sure you stock up the house with food and all the things you need. Because, it's about to go down, Shorty. The only way this deal won't take place is if you rat us out. If you do, the saying that will apply to you and the fam will be snitches get stitches or in this case snitches will get destroyed," he expresses forcefully and makes an explosive booming sound as he dramatically widens his hands.

"You are a clown," the spy says laughing and shaking his head.

"Remember, I am a businesswoman myself, so let me make sure this is a favorable deal and that I have considered every detail in our agreement. Ok, I will be saved, and my family will be saved. Ok, what about protection if someone disregards the scarlet red cord hanging on the outside of my window," Rahab inquires as she walks around with folded arms and biting her nails.

"They will die if they harm you or your family, because the scarlet red cord is a symbol that you are protected by The Man. I don't think anybody wants that work, right there," he assures confidently nodding his head and standing in that buff position again.

The two spies eagerly watch Rahab consider their proposition and wait for her to respond.

"Mmmm, I guess you got yourself a deal. Let's shake on it," she states with a big smile extending her hand.

Rahab and the spy A.K.A Love of Her Life kiss, get married and have a baby named Boaz.

Shopping Mall

The ladies are soooo engaged listening to Rahab's story.

"Girl, shut up! That's how you and hubby met, got married and that's why you love red ribbons?" Wella asks with excitement and awe.

"Mmmm, *he thought you were worth saving*, Chil," she snickers as she sings and sips on her drink.

"The scarlet red ribbon represents the blood of Christ which is your protection from the enemy," Mary explains while praising God.

"My family and I were protected and death passed us over because the red scarlet cord represents the blood of the lamb," Rahab explains emotionally wiping a tear from her eye.

Gomer gently rubs Rahab's back.

"My life changed forever on that day because God thought enough of lil' ol' me, prostitute Rahab to spare my life. God orchestrated all of those events, while I was still caught up in my mess to deliver me and my family. That blows my mind every time I think about it. He blessed me even while I was hoeing and not keeping my body holy. Who does that?" Rahab cries from her core.

"I know what you mean! Please stop because you are making me cry too. God will forgive and forget your past, because he doesn't keep records of wrongs but some people do," Gomer says wiping a tear from her eye.

"When people saw that I was no longer available for them to get their rocks off, I lost street credibility. People thought that I thought I was better than them, because I married an officer and a gentleman. Yep, I did change. I changed drastically for the better. So, people perceptions of me don't even matter," Rahab admits as the tears stop flowing from her eyes.

The ladies leave the mall and decide to have a slumber party. They change into their pajamas, order food, and eat in their luxurious room.

Chapter 23

Just A Slipping and Backsliding

> "I will heal their backsliding I will love them freely,
> for my anger has turned away from him."
> -Hosea 14:4 NKJV

Country Club

"These wings are so good. I am loving our heartfelt conversations… they're so good and so informative. Gomer, please share with us something that we don't know about you. Of course, we know you were a woman of the night, evening, and day just like Rahab but give us details. Inquiring minds want to know the real real, Sis," Wella encourages as she smacks on her wings.

Everybody begins laughing and nodding their heads agreeing with Wella.

"I remember when I was pregnant with Boaz, and I was feeding my cravings while I was sitting on the sofa. I turns on the TV and guess who I see on Jerry Springer. None other than our girl, Gomer," Rahab dramatically shares falling out of her chair laughing.

Mary and Wella are perplexed while Gomer looks at Rahab with a straight face and shakes her head.

"Stoppp playyyiing," Mary says slowly announcing every syllable slowly.

"Upp! Are you playing or are you for real?" Wella chuckles with her hand over her mouth.

Gomer puts her hand over her forehead with her head faced down.

"Rahab will never let me live this down. So, let me just go right on and tell you," Gomer shares to satisfy the girls curiosity.

Gomer sits up in a comfortable position and folds her legs in cross-legged fashion.

"Ok, what had happened was, Eddie Murphy and Martin Lawrence's *Life* was being promoted errrywhere! I am not sure if the Jerry Springer Show was assisting in marketing, sponsorship or what, but the topic like always had to deal with something related to paternity. This particular episode was titled "Who's The Baby Daddy."The introduction started with the scene of the movie Life where, the white warden's daughter gets pregnant and has a black baby. The warden lines up all of the prisoners, holds up the baby next to each one of their faces to determine if one of them could be the possible father of his grand baby. The inmates know that "Can't Get Right" is the actual father of the baby but instead each inmate claims that they are the father of dat there baby to cover for "Can't Get Right." I was so embarrassed when I saw the introduction of the show on which I was a guest. I had no idea that I would receive so much attention from that show, and I also didn't know who the baby father was. So I went on the show thinking that it was an easy way to get a paternity test without having to spend money," Gomer explains shrugging her shoulders in regret of her past.

"I am definitely not judging you, because I don't have any room to do so, but what made you become so promiscuous in the first place. Now, I have laid all my dirt on line, and it's a part of my past. So, tell me your story," Wella says itching to find out about Gomer's past.

"Well since you all must know; I got it from my mama. When I was younger my mother used to have a raisin cake stand. I am not sure if it was a business front or what. Now, the raisin cake recipe has been in my family for years, and it has been passed down to my generation. Somewhat, like my desire to trick," she admits calmly with a straight face.

The ladies cover their mouths while trying their best not to laugh.

"I can't, I just can't do it! I guess I am going to be the one who addresses this elephant in the room. So, Gomer what you telling me is that your mommy…..passed down her tricking recipe to you," Rahab leans in, puts her arm around Gomer's shoulder and dies laughing.

The ladies all laugh uncontrollably falling out and holding their stomachs.

"Yup, this is my story," she smiles and chuckles but not hysterically like the others.

"So, tell us about Hosea. I absolutely love the way he treats you," Mary compliments as she smiles and wipes her hands and mouth with a napkin.

"Hosea is such a sweetheart! You know how you meet some men and you have to go out of your way to try to impress them. Naw, not my Hosea. He is definitely not that type. He loves me exactly for me and while I was still in my mess he was loving me. When we had gotten married I was still out in the streets and messing with every Tom, Dick, and Harry. Despite not being considered or deemed wife material by society, he still took a chance on a girl like me. He knew my lifestyle and still decided to make me his wife. His father loves me like a daughter and thought that I was perfect for his son. Now, his father keeps his ear to the streets, and he knew about my past as well. I hurt Hosea so deeply at times, because I was selfish and addicted to my loose behavior. I brought all that junk into our house, and he definitely did not deserve it. All he wanted to do and still desires to do is to love me wholeheartedly. When I went on The Jerry Springer Show for the paternity test, it was because I wasn't sure if my baby was Hosea's. Everybody around town would make jokes about him when they saw me walking around with my pregnant belly and holding his hand. People called him all sorts of names and thought that he was a truly weak man, because he still treated me like a queen. They thought he was whipped sexually, but that didn't have anything to do with it. Well, I don't think. Ok, maybe he was whipped also. You know when I think about it, Hosea still benefits from my old lifestyle today, if you know what I mean. When I was roaming around town, and it was rumored that my son could possibly not be his child, Hosea was going to divorce me. We did separate momentarily but thank God that he decided to still keep me as his wife. His father had told him to go get your wife, love her and he did just that. Hosea's love for me is a replica of how Christ loves us despite our sinful nature. He forgives us and loves us wholeheartedly. Nothing can separate us from his love! Hosea was able to love me despite my flaws, because his first love is God, not me and definitely not his ego. When a man doesn't know God or have a personal relationship with him, that means he doesn't know love. Therefore, he can't possibly love you right! I am not sitting up here trying to make you believe that Hosea is perfect, because he's not. But, he knows how to repent and get right back on track with the Lord after making mistakes. All I am saying is, that he knows how to allow God to lead him and to love me with the love of the Lord. Don't you know that love covers a multitude of sins as it says in 1 Peter 4:8? Booyah! Now, that's grace, mercy, and favor at its finest for y'all, hoes," Gomer stands up raises her voice, hits the table, and raises both of her hands with a mug on her face like she is playing a game of dominos.

"Rahab, you is a fool! It seems like Hosea is giving you that real good love. I ain't mad at you! Now, that's that type of love every woman should desire when making their list of things that they want in their husband. That real love should be number one! Now look y'all! Everyone up in here has told their story except for Mary…Mary quite contrary. Is it that you are trying to save the best for last or please tell us what's up. How did you become all holy and sanctified cause you was a hot mess when we first met?" Wella boldly asks with one hand on her hip and her head rolling.

Chapter 24

But You Don't Know The Cost

"I tell you, her sins- and they are many- have been forgiven, so she has shown me much love."
-Luke 7:47 ESV

Mary looks out the window as if she never heard a word that Wella said.

"Ladies, how are you enjoying the wings? I am enjoying mine. I am definitely not saving the best for last, but the worst for last. You all remember how I was 'bout it 'bout it in these streets."

"Ummm, not really! I think that statement is way over the top and totally overrated. I'm just saying if you ask me," Rahab contemplates with her hand on her chin and then shrugs her shoulders.

Wella and Gomer are drinking and eating and try not to spit out the food from their mouths while laughing so hard.

"Girl, you know if I wanted it, it was mine and it didn't matter who it belonged to. Back in the day, my sister Martha, the goodie two shoes of the family, was always making sure that the house was straight, cooking, looking after our brother Lazarus and making sure daddy's business was handled. I on the other hand, was running the streets," Mary says as she reminisces about her life.

Mary and Martha's House

Martha, a thin 28 year old woman with a cappuccino hue and tiny waist bursts into Mary's room while Young Mary, a 25 year old woman with a cocoa brown complexion wearing the latest hairstyle and fashion, is listening to music and texting on her phone.

"Lazarus, it's time to take your medicine. Mary, clean up your room now. It looks a mess in here and is starting to smell," Martha states angrily with one hand holding the door open and with one finger pointing at Mary.

"Martha, I am not playing with you. Get out of my room now and if you want it cleaned, clean it yourself," Mary yells, hops off her bed and goes to kitchen to grab five freshly baked cookies that Martha made.

"Mary, you are lazy and greedy! You don't help with anything around here! It is always about you! You are so selfish, but you are going to learn," Martha expresses, walks away, and shakes her head.

"But who is going to teach me?! Yeah, I thought so. Not a word because you know what's best for you," Mary raises her voice, looks at Martha sternly and stuffs her mouth with a cookie.

Mary runs out the door and jumps into her convertible Mercedes Benz.

Jasper's Restaurant

She rolls up to Jaspers in Largo, Maryland to meet her friends for happy hour. Rare Essence is playing with Mrs. Kim on the mic when she walks into the restaurant. She waves at Kim and winks at her while she is singing.

"We got Mary up in the building partying with us tonight," Kim melodically raps while holding up her glass acknowledging Mary's presence.

Mary holds up her glass and winks at Kim. Mary walks to her seat and makes the people move who are sitting in her designated booth.

"Y'all know better, so get up out of my seat. You know who I am! So, when you see me coming, you need to move and put some respect on it. Don't let it happen again or there are going to be consequences and repercussions. You know who I am, and you know I don't play," Mary informs loudly while holding her drink in her hand.

The people move from her table, and Mary asks for two orders of buffalo hot wings and shrimp and grits. While she was eating all of the food and sharing one order of wings with her friends, she notices a young lady in her early twenties with an athletic build and a gorgeous smile that lights up the room. Mrs. Kim comes down from the stage to greet her with a huge hug. The bartender and waitress go over to meet her to take her order. She daps up and hugs several people who are at Jasper's that night. This lady named Kisha, has a fine chocolate man take off her coat before she sits down in her booth. The waitress makes sure Kisha's booth and table are clean and waiting. Kisha takes off her exclusive Gucci bag that was just showcased during the most recent New York Fashion week. She catches Mary's full attention.

Country Club

"Before I go any further, I wanted to let you know that I was hanging with the wrong crowd back then. I was hanging with Jezebel a.k.a. Jeze who was extremely off her rocker and a treacherous bully and a killer. This chic had bodies on her, and I was hanging with her y'all. Why are you acting like you don't remember who she is? I mean who she was. Remember, she was all over the news for dying horrifically. She was thrown out of a window and eaten by dogs. Don't you remember that? I guess what they say must be true in some instances, if you live by the sword you die by the sword. She was into to a lot of bad things. Don't you know that men were even scared of her and even men in powerful positions. She was crazzzzy! So, I thought it was best to have a chic like that on my team instead of going against her. Then, I also was rolling with Delilah the irresistible seducer. She had body and luscious lips for days, and the men could not turn her down. She was known for setting men up, getting them either hemmed up or even worse. Y'all, don't remember her either? She was also on the news for having something to do with Samson's killing. She seduced him and set him up for men to capture and torture him. Samson was the man… and was so powerful. The brothas were jealous of him and devised a plan to shut him down. That was really sad! I was also hanging out with that girl who was known for lying. What was her name? I can't remember. She was also on the news for rolling on her baby and suffocating him while she was sleep. Then, there was another lady who was living with her who had just given birth to a baby at the same time as she did. She switched the babies to make it seem like the baby that was alive belonged to her and the dead baby was the other woman's. She sure knew how to create a lie but was eventually found guilty. These are the woman that I chose to hang out with back in the day," Mary explains to help the ladies get a clear picture of the connections she had.

The ladies acknowledged that they remembered hearing or reading something about these women's stories.

"So, I started to ask my crew about the girl and guy who were getting way more attention that I was," Mary says picking up where she left off.

Jasper's Restaurant

Mary leans over and asks her friend inquisitively, "Mmmm, who are they and why haven't I seen them before"?

"Oh, since you been summer vacationing in the Hamptons and have been in and out of the country, Kisha and her hubby have been frequenting this spot. Please tell me you don't remember Kisha from high school, who used to smile all the time. She left a few years ago but has moved back in the area," Jeze explains to Mary as Mary stuffs her face and stares at the couple.

"This next round of drinks and food are on me," Kisha stands up on stage and announces on the mic with a huge grin.

"Oh, I see, this chic thinks she's the one. Kisha thinks she is like that and I don't like her. I am paying for our food. We don't need her handouts. Tell me more about her. How is she able to afford that mega bill she is handling?" Mary asks with envy speaking between bites.

"Thanks, big baller for paying for the wings you ordered for us to share. Yeah, back to ol' girl. Kisha's husband has his own business that is doing pretty good. I don't believe she works neither. He takes real good care of her and spoils her. She lives in a big house, drives a nice car, and dresses her butt off. She doesn't want for nothing. I don't know her, but she smiles to dang much. It's quite irritating if you ask me. But… she did hit the jackpot, because her man is fine," Jeze hatefully explains to Mary while looking in Kisha's direction.

Mary nods, grits, rolls her eyes and they leave the restaurant. Mary researches Kisha's social media accounts to find out all the information she possibly can about Kisha, her life, and her man. Kisha has left a trail of history for Mary to determine Kisha's daily whereabouts as well as her man's weekly schedule enabling her to conjure up an evil plan.

"So, Kisha thinks she is all of that does she. She ain't even all that anyway. She looks alright, and she ain't even wearing her real hair on these pics. Yep, I bet you she is bald headed that's why she is wearing those beautiful lace fronts. Ugh! I can't stand her, and she is always smiling. I wonder what that fine man, she's got, sees in her and why he does all that stuff for her. Kisha's shape ain't even all that. She doesn't even have a butt. Yeah, I got something for that tail," Mary smirks wickedly while staring at Kisha's picture on social media.

Mary creates a group FaceTime chat with Jezebel, Delilah and the lying chic. She decides to designate rolls and assignments to the ladies to destroy Kisha's peace of mind as well as take the smile off of her face.

"So, ladies… thank you for taking time out of your busy schedules to join me on a mission to destroy Kisha. What she is not going to do is think she is going to come up in my town and take my place. After searching her social media accounts intricately, I see that she spends plenty of time with her family. Her son runs for the Glenarden track club and Kisha and her husband attend those practices. The practices look like, from her posting date, they are scheduled, Monday through Thursday with track meets on Saturdays. Delilah, I would like you to go to the track practices dressed to impress, entice her man, and steal him. Play with Kisha's mind, make her feel insecure and wreak havoc on their household. I know this is right up your alley. My lying friend, I need you to do what you do best. I see that Kisha has several followers on her social media pages, therefore I want you to tell lies that make her look bad, destroy her reputation and relationships and cause baby mama drama. You know, like what you do best. I want you to embarrass her and make her feel worthless by any means necessary. Jeze you already know what to do! Make her life a living nightmare! I want you to threaten her by sending messages that scare the heck out of her! I want you to tell her that she better move out of her house, she better give up her man, and all her belongings if she wants her child to live or if she wants to see another day. This operation is no different from all of the others! Destroy that chic's peace of mind, her will to live and remove that dang smile off of her face," Mary yells as she gives direct instructions and bangs on the table in front of her.

Delilah, Jeze and the liar agree to do their assignments with smiles on their faces and rubbing their hands together. They get started immediately.

Glenarden Track Practice

While Kisha's son is at track practice with his father, Delilah bends over in front of Kisha's husband wearing booty shorts with the voluptuous sides of her cheeks hanging out. Kisha's husband scratches his head and pokes out his lips admiring the size and shape of Delilah's peach Delilah feels wandering eyes pressing her in the small of her back, so she stands up and turns around. Delilah sparks a conversation with Kisha's husband with her luscious lips accentuated by red lipstick, and they both enjoy obviously flirting with each other. When Kisha arrives, she notices her husband talking to Delilah and walks towards them. When Delilah notices Kisha approaching, she says hey to Kisha with a chuckle and walks away slowly. Delilah continues to come the next few practices and attempts to get under Kisha's skin by not speaking to her. One day, Kisha arrives at practice to meet her husband who was already there. Delilah intentionally stands next to Kisha and her husband to play mental games. Kisha's husband greets his wife by saying hey babe and simultaneously Delilah and Kisha respond with a hey. Kisha looks at Delilah with a mug to let her know to stop playing. Kisha looks at her husband, but he plays like he is Doh Doh the Fool. Kisha's husband and Delilah begin sleeping with each other occasionally. Mary even has sex with him because he is fine as ever.

Evil Plans at Work

In churning the rumor mill on the social media platforms, the liar begins to plant seeds of discord. She posts pictures everywhere with a caption that states," Kisha is the poster child for what a gold digger looks like." This liar hacks all of Kisha's social media accounts and posts Kisha friends' pictures publicly with negative messages about them. The liar creates a horrible reputation for Kisha that makes people think Kisha thinks that she is better them. Some of Kisha's friends began to separate from her because they believe what the posts say. Kisha's son doesn't want to play sports anymore, because his mental state has been impacted by all of this drama. The son stops respecting Kisha as his stepmother because of the negative things his biological mother is telling him about Kisha.

Jeze sends her goons to tell Kisha that she better, if she knows what is in her best interest, leave her husband, child, home, car, and her entire lifestyle as she is currently living. Jeze torments and explains that she wants it all, no if, and or buts about it. Jeze feels Kisha is not worthy of this lifestyle and doesn't even deserve it….especially not the man. Jeze feels Kisha is not good enough for him, but Jeze has someone else who is a better fit for him.

Jasper's Restaurant

The next night the girls drive their separate cars to go to happy hour, and Kisha and hubby walk up in the restaurant styling and profiling per usual. Kisha steps on the stage.

"Drinks and food for everyone," Kisha states and smiles as she walks off the stage.

"This chic really doesn't know how to quit. Does she? She is not like the other ones who are now running around like chickens with their heads cut off," Mary laughs while moving her arms up and down like a chicken.

They all fall out laughing.

"Naw, she is still with her man, living her best life with that beautiful smile. I can always put a hit out on her. You just say the word," Jeze expresses while pointing her fingers in the shape of a gun in Kisha's direction.

Kisha walks to the ladies room and Mary follows close behind her. When Mary walks into the bathroom, she stares at Kisha who is washing her hands and looking into the mirror. Mary washes her hands in the sink next to Kisha and looks in the mirror in front of her. Kisha looks at Mary.

"How are you doing Mary?" Kisha smirks and shakes her head.

Mary does not respond.

"It's fine. You don't have to say word. I know what you and your girls are doing. You have been doing this child's play since high school. You target an individual and try, and I mean try, to destroy their life and cause fear. Let me ask you, do you know who my father is? Clearly you don't now, but you will see clearly. I am praying for you and I forgive you," Kisha informs calmly and elegantly touching Mary's shoulder as she dries her hands with a paper towel. Mary looks in the mirror and is baffled after reflecting on Kisha's words.

Mary's Transformation

Mary leaves the bathroom and tells her posse that she is retiring for the night. Mary leaves abruptly, goes to her car and turns the ignition. The radio station 104.1 Praise begins to play the song *Just for Me* by Karen Clark Sheard. Mary listens for a minute, turns quickly to a station that she has never heard before on XM Satellite. On Kirk Franklin's Praise, a song by Yolanda Adams called *Open My Heart* is playing on the radio. For the next week everything that the girls attempt to do to Kisha fall back on them. Delilah's man is cheating on her with another woman whom she knows, who's butt and physique look better than hers. The liar's reputation is destroyed, because people tell the truth about the way the liar steals from others. Also, she ends up being featured on America's Most Wanted for her past crimes. Jeze is thrown out of a window and eaten by dogs.

Mary's mind is playing tricks on her for all the evil and wickedness that she has done to people over the years. She can't sleep at night, because she believes that she is next in line to receive intense punishment for what she did to Kisha. Every time she turns on the radio, it seems like a gospel message is directed towards her. For some reason, her radio station always turns to a gospel channel without her guidance. One day, she wakes up, looks in the mirror and decides that she can't take it anymore. She grabs hold of Lazarus' medicines, prescribed to cure his infection, in efforts to overdose and commit suicide. She hears voices in her head telling her that she is not worthy and that she should just kill herself. The voices keep getting louder and louder telling her to do it. She goes to her car and begins to drive and sees several stop signs but proceeds through them without stopping. A police officer signals her to pull over. Mary obeys his signal and pulls over. The police officer walks to Mary's car on the driver's side. Mary rolls down her window and begins to pull out her license.

"Mary, I don't need your driver's license or to check your record. I have been following you for years. So, today I finally got your attention. Open the door and get out of the driver's seat," he says politely as he opens the door for Mary.

"I am videotaping this whole conversation. I am just letting you know. How did you know my name and why are you following me?" Mary asks frantically as she steps out of the car.

"I am not one of those officers. I want to talk to you. Mary I have seen the things you have done to people like

Kisha and a host of many others. Everybody except for Kisha gave up on life, became mentally ill or committed suicide. The devil comes to kill, steal, and destroy. He has been using you to do his dirty work for him. The reason why your tactics haven't worked on Kisha and she is still smiling brightly is because of her relationship with her father. I know you can't see it but Kisha husband's wandering eye, adultery and dealing with the drama of all the things come with being married to him keeps her close to the father. The highlight reel that she is posting on social media does not reflect the reality of her life. Mary, what you can't actually stand about Kisha is her light! The light you see in her is me which means you are rejecting me! You are in darkness, but today I am going to bring you out. Mary you come from a family that is well off financially, you have a nice home, clothes, and go on lavish vacations, but you are still not happy. Kisha allowed me to fill her void. I can do the same thing for you if you allow me, and your life will never be the same again. Come eat and drink. It's on me! I got it! All you have to do is open your heart and let me in," the police officer said compassionately holding out his hand.

Tears stream from Mary's eyes as she hugs the officer and begins to cry her eyes out.

"Sometimes, it takes some people hitting rock bottom before they can see me clearly," he says while embracing Mary tightly.

"I am so sorry for all the wrong that I have done especially to people like Kisha who don't deserve it," Mary says while crying with snot running from her nose.

"You are going to do great things, and I am going to use you mightily. Now, give Lazarus his medicine back," the man says looking at Mary from the corner of his eyes.

When Mary looks up, the officer is gone as well as his car and she still has her arms in the embracing position. Although, she can't see him anymore she feels his warmth in her heart. Mary is never the same after that encounter.

Country Club

"Hopefully, all of you have a better understanding of why I am the way you see me now. I have come a mighty long way, and it was all because of God's grace. I'm so glad that God delivered me from those deadly sins that I was committing. Sloth, gluttony, greed, lust, pride, envy, and wrath were all inside of my heart. I'm so grateful that God delivered me, because I do not know where I would be if it had not been for the Lord on my side. My worship is for real! I washed Jesus' with my tears because he has forgiven and delivered me from so much. When I worship and praise God y'all, I don't care who is watching. Shucks, hopefully they will join me! He has been sooo good to me! My relationship with Martha has improved for the better, because we understand and respect each other's boundaries. She knows not to invade my space when I am worshiping and sitting at the feet of

Jesus. Also, I began to help her clean more except when the presence of the Lord is in the house. Kisha and I became close friends. She often gives me godly counsel and helps me to comprehend the things of God which confuse me sometimes. Kisha still has challenges in her marriage but chooses to walk upright before her husband just like it says in 1 Peter 3:1-4. He eventually gained a closer relationship with Christ. Sooo, this is my story and I am sticking to it!" Mary exclaims throwing her hands up in the air praising the Lord.

The ladies were in awe. Gomer falls out on the floor laughing.

"I am still trying to wrap my head around this…our Mary being straight gangsta," Gomer hollers and falls out on the floor again.

"Now I would have expected that reaction right there from Rahab. Y'all, I am not perfect and there is much room for improvement. I am so thankful that I am not what I used to be," Mary states with tears falling from eyes her hands still lifted up in praise.

Wella, Rahab, and Gomer join Mary in worshipping the Lord. They enjoy the rest of their girl's trip, but when their getaway is over they allow the Lord to take the steering wheel.

Chapter 25

Saving A Wretch Like Me

"Blessed are those who hunger and thirst for righteousness, for they shall be satisfied."
-Matthew 5:6 ESV

Correctional Facility

"That concludes my story telling today. I have left a tract of helpful scriptures and free Bibles to assist you with getting to know the Lord better. Every story that was discussed here today is in the Bible. I just retold the stories with a modern day twist and modern imagery. I have also included scriptures in the tract for your reference whenever you need them. Before I leave, I do have a question for you. Is anyone hungry and thirsty for righteousness? It's already been paid for, and you definitely can get your fill for free right here and right now. Remember you are not alone and we have all sinned and fallen short of the glory of God. You need Him. I need Him. We need him," Deborah explains from her heart as she extends the invitation to salvation.

Cassandra eyes begin to tear up. Niecy puts her arm around Cassandra's shoulders and whispers in her ear.

"Girl, you aren't the only one and you are not alone. I was the same way as you when I gave my life to Jesus Christ. Cassandra don't fight or resist, Sis. Give God what He wants and that's you Boo," Niecy speaks convincingly to Cassandra as tears roll down her eyes.

Cassandra gives her life to Christ and her sisters in Christ applaud.

"You have made the best decision in your life and your life will never be the same after today. The ladies who are sitting in this circle with you today have already made the same decision you have just made. I am so proud of you, Sis! Cassandra you are free, Love! You are no longer bound because where the spirit of the Lord is there is liberty! Hallelujah!" Deborah shouts and praises the Lord.

Soooo, this whole time y'all might have thought my girls, Cassandra and Niecy, were locked up in jail… did you? Tell the truth and shame the devil! To be honest, they did need correction as we all do throughout our spiritual journey of life. But, let me spill the tea or in other words, here's the 411. Cassandra, Niecey and the other ladies were corrected and changed in the facility at the Women's Conference hosted in the DMV. The guest speaker Deborah delivered a spirit filled message creatively that penetrated the hearts of the attendees. The ladies were filled up with spiritual clarity, freed from mental bondage and lifted from under the weights that were holding them down. The women were encouraged to live their best lives ever.

A Queen's Reflection

A Queen's Reflection is broken up into three sections, **A Queen with a Past,**

A Struggling Queen, and A Queen with a Future.

A Queen with a Past is for queens who have overcome being involved in situations similar to our sisters mentioned in the book. A Struggling Queen is for queens who are currently entangled in and enduring these kind of relationships, who are trying to figure things out and need some help in this area. A Queen with a Future is your private time-out to think about the Queen, The Daughter you want to be as you move past trials and situations that you experienced.

Sis, this is a judgement free zone, but it does require your complete honesty with yourself on where you are spiritually and mentally.

A Queen with a Past

1. Have you ever been in any situations as these women mentioned in this book? If it was a past situation you endured, how did you overcome?

2. In hindsight, what attracted and drew you to this type of relationship? What void were you attempting to fill?
3. What did you learn about yourself from these experiences?
4. What gave you the strength to leave and not return to these type of relationships? How did you overcome?
5. What advice would you give, how would you support a dear sister queen struggling with any of these situations?

Queen, please write your answers to create your personal testimony and include your success tips that you've utilized to overcome. When lead by God, please intentionally share with our sisters who are still struggling in these areas we have overcome. Then, let's persistently pray on a regular basis for our sister queens who are still struggle dealing with their self-worth and are challenged in their relationships.

A Struggling Queen

1. Have you ever been or are you currently in situations like any of the women mentioned in this book? If you are currently involved in situations described in this book, what void is this type of relationship filling for you?
2. Did something happen in your past that draws you to the types of relationships that are shared in Daughters of the King? If so, what did you experience?

3. How do you think your life would change without these type of relationships? How would it affect you to leave them alone?

A Queen With A Future

Sis, you are a queen that is soooo worthy of real love from one man – instead of just getting some of your needs met from multiple partners.

1. Have you prayed and asked Jesus to help you in these areas? Queen, He already knows all about it and wants to help you. The King is waiting on you with open arms!
2. Picture who you are as the Daughter of The King you are called to be. Write about your vision of who is this queen and how she shows up in her own life and in the lives of others.

Sis, Listen to Lisa McClendon's Who Can Love You More (Live) The words of this song is soooo true!

Then, please pray the scriptures that I have included in the Daughters of the King Tract (in the back of the book) that are pertinent to your situation. Personalize the scriptures by putting your name in as you read them. In addition, therapy may also be a good option for you. Sometimes we all need a little extra help! I love you and remember you are not alone! I am praying for you and yes Queen you are an overcomer, too!

Daughters of the King Tract

Story References

Eve's Story/Adam and Eve – Genesis 2:4-3:24

Bathsheba's Story/David and Bathsheba - 2 Samuel 11, 12

Wella's Story/Samaritan Woman at the Well - John 4

Rahab Story/The Red Rope of Redemption - Joshua 2

Gomer's Story/Hosea and Gomer - Hosea 1-3

Mary's Story/Mary Magdalene - Luke 8:1-3; Mark 16:9; John 20:16; Luke 7:36-50; Luke 10:38, 39; John 11:1, 2; John 12: 1-8; Matthew 27: 55, 56, 60-61; John 19:25; John 20:1,2, 18, Matthew 28:7; Luke 24:9-10

Scriptures on Love

Romans 5:8 ESV

"But God shows his love for us in that while we were still sinners, Christ died for us."

Psalm 86:15 ESV

"But you, O Lord, are a God merciful and gracious, slow to anger and abounding in steadfast love and faithfulness."

Romans 8:38:39 ESV

"For I am sure that neither death nor life, nor angels nor rulers, nor things present nor things to come, nor powers, nor height nor depth, nor anything else in all creation, will be able to separate us from the love of God in Christ Jesus our Lord."

Scriptures on Repentance

1 John 1:9 ESV

"If we confess our sins, he is faithful and just to forgive us our sins and to cleanse us from all unrighteousness."

Acts 3:19 ESV

"Repent therefore, and turn again, that your sins may be blotted out,"

2 Peter 3:9 ESV

"The Lord is not slow to fulfill his promise as some count slowness, but is patient toward you, not wishing that any should perish, but that all should reach repentance."

Scriptures on Forgiveness

Ephesians 1:7 ESV

"In him we have redemption through his blood, the forgiveness of our trespasses, according to the riches of his grace,"

Colossians 3:13 ESV

"Bearing with one another and, if one has a complaint against another, forgiving each other; as the Lord has forgiven you, so you also must forgive."

Isaiah 1:18 ESV

"Come now, let us reason together, says the Lord: though your sins are like scarlet, they shall be as white as snow; though they are red like crimson, they shall become like wool."

Scriptures on Deliverance

Luke 10:19 ESV

"Behold, I have given you authority to tread on serpents and scorpions, and over all the power of the enemy, and nothing shall hurt you."

1 Corinthians 10:13 ESV

"No temptation has overtaken you that is not common to man. God is faithful, and he will not let you be tempted beyond your ability, but with the temptation he will also provide the way of escape, that you may be able to endure it."

Colossians 1:13 ESV

"He has delivered us from the domain of darkness and transferred us to the kingdom of his beloved Son,"

Psalm 40:20 ESV

"He drew me up from the pit of destruction, out of the miry bog, and set my feet upon a rock, making my steps secure."

Psalm 107:20 ESV

"He sent out his word and healed them and delivered them from their destruction."

Psalm 34:4 ESV

"I sought the Lord, and he answered me and delivered me from all my fears."

Scriptures on Guilt and Shame

Romans 3:23 NKJV

"For all have sinned and fall short of the glory of God,"

Romans 8:1 ESV

"There is therefore now no condemnation for those who are in Christ Jesus."

John 3:17 ESV

"For God did not send his Son into the world to condemn the world, but in order that the world might be saved through him."

Please always remember the following concerning yourself:

Luke 4:18 ESV

"The Spirit of the Lord is upon me, because he has anointed me to proclaim good news to the poor. He has sent me to proclaim liberty to the captives and recovering of sight to the blind, to set at liberty those who are oppressed,"

www.ingramcontent.com/pod-product-compliance
Lightning Source LLC
Chambersburg PA
CBHW061146170426
43209CB00011B/1570